The Time of Revolt

The Time of Revolt

Donatella Di Cesare

Translated by David Broder

polity

Originally published as *Il tempo della rivolta* © Bollati Boringhieri editore, Torino, 2020

This English edition © Polity Press, 2022

Polity Press
65 Bridge Street
Cambridge CB2 1UR, UK

Polity Press
101 Station Landing
Suite 300
Medford, MA 02155, USA

ISBN-13: 978-1-5095-4838-5
ISBN-13: 978-1-5095-4839-2 (paperback)

A catalogue record for this book is available from the British Library.

Library of Congress Control Number: 2021939487

Typeset in 11 on 14 Adobe Garamond
by Fakenham Prepress Solutions, Fakenham, Norfolk NR21 8NL
Printed and bound in Great Britain by CPI Group (UK) Ltd, Croydon

The publisher has used its best endeavours to ensure that the URLs for external websites referred to in this book are correct and active at the time of going to press. However, the publisher has no responsibility for the websites and can make no guarantee that a site will remain live or that the content is or will remain appropriate.

Every effort has been made to trace all copyright holders, but if any have been overlooked the publisher will be pleased to include any necessary credits in any subsequent reprint or edition.

For further information on Polity, visit our website:
politybooks.com

Contents

CONTENTS

My hope is the last breath …
My flight is revolt,
My heaven the abyss of tomorrow.
Heiner Müller, 'The Angel of Despair'[1]

1 Heiner Müller, 'Three Angels', in Gerhard Fischer (ed.), *The Mudrooroo/Müller Project*. Kensington: New South Wales University Press, 1993, p. 45.

The Right to Breathe

Revolt is breaking out all over the world. It flares up, it peters out, then it continues its spread once more. It crosses borders, it rocks nations, it agitates continents. A glance at the map of its sudden outbreaks and countless eruptions reveals its intermittent advance across the bumpy political landscape of the new century. Its vast scale is matched only by its intensity. Its topography outlines a landscape in which confrontation turns to opposition, discord and open struggle. Protests spread, acts of disobedience multiply, and clashes intensify. This is the time of revolt.

The blaze of revolt may seem short-lived, the event fleeting. But revolt ought not to be considered merely ephemeral. Through all its surges and retreats, it comprises a global phenomenon, and one which promises to endure. Not even the pandemic has been able to put out the flames. At a moment when many were already reflecting on the disappearance of the *pólis* and the loss of public space, revolt resurfaced, overwhelming and uncontainable. It surged forth from Buenos Aires to Hong Kong, from Rio de Janeiro to Beirut, and from London to Bangkok.

The fuse of a fresh explosion was lit in Minneapolis. George Floyd's final words, spoken as his executioner continued to suffocate him – 'I can't breathe' – have become emblematic. The importance of these words is no accident but owes to a coincidence revealed by the secret synchronism of history. George Floyd's terrible death was the result not of the virus stopping him from breathing but, rather, the work of a racist tyranny perpetrated through police techniques.

Suddenly, the right to breathe appeared in all its existential and political significance. 'I can't breathe' rose up as the battle-hymn of revolt – both an accusation against the abuse of power and a denunciation of that asphyxiating system which steals the breath away.[1] In capital's compulsive vortex – that catastrophic spiral that has turned the right to breathe into a privilege for the few – what comes to the fore is breathlessness of the exploited, those who have to submit to an accelerated, relentless rhythm, the most vulnerable, confined to an oppressive, anxious scarcity. 'I can't breathe' has thus become the slogan that claims the right to breathe – the political right to exist.

But the killing of George Floyd is one of a long series of abuses that the forces of order have perpetrated using similar methods – often termed the 'excessive use of force'. One commonplace notion holds that the police legitimately resort to violence in response to some other, prior violence. On this reading, as the police impose control, as they seek to pacify things, it is inevitable that a misstep will be made, that excesses will occur. Any resulting discrimination thus appears as an unavoidable anomaly, the malfunctioning of an otherwise correct system built on equality. But is this really the case? Or is the malfunction itself systematic – providing a glimpse of the fundamental workings of an inscrutable institution?

Abuses by police arouse such boundless indignation because they appear not as mere accidents but, rather, as revelatory acts – the tip of the iceberg for a whole system of violence built on discrimination. On the one hand there are blacks, and on the other whites; on the one hand the poor, and on the other the rich; and so on. So, these abuses are no mere anomalous application of the rules but the functioning of a mechanism that defines the political order. The police draw boundaries, choose, discriminate, allow some into the centre and push others back to the margins. For this reason, there is something rather misleading about an economistic reading that sees the police's job only as a matter of normalization for the sake of increasing the wealth of the few.[2] Rather, the question of policing is part of the economy of public space. For this is where the right to belong and to appear is determined: who is allowed access, to circulate freely, to feel at home, and who is profiled, intimidated, chased into zones of invisibility, if not even jailed? There can be no denying the police's segregationist use of power. This is a means of more or less brutally consolidating the supremacy of some – but isn't this itself racism, state xenophobia? – and sharpening differences, which it makes plain for all to see.

This is not to say that the police are illegal. Rather, they are authorized by law to carry out extra-legal functions. They do not stop at *administering* the law but constantly re-establish its boundaries. Walter Benjamin speaks of the 'ignominious' aspect of the police as an institution, situated in the ambiguous sphere where all distinction between the violence that founds the law and the violence that maintains it disappears.[3] This ambivalence also helps to explain the police's juridical extraterritoriality, which makes them an exceptional case even within the logic of institutional power. In short, the police monopolize the interpretation of violence, for they redefine the norms of their own actions and, appealing to 'security', increase their grip over individuals' lives. Their violent sovereignty is as slippery as it is spectral.

For this reason, instances of police violence are no mere anomalies but reveal this institution's dark, opaque foundations. These outrages are like snapshots which capture the police as they conquer space, take power over bodies, examine and experiment with a new form of legality, as they redefine the limits of the possible. If these scenes are the cause of such indignation, if they seem so 'ignominious', it is because they are the sign of an authoritarian power, the proof of the undeniable existence of a police state within the state of law (*Rechtsstaat*).

In this light, just as these acts of violence reveal the true essence of the police, they also shed light on the architecture of a politics which captures and banishes, includes and excludes. This is an architecture in which discrimination is always already latent. Suddenly we can see the borders of immunodemocracy, where the defence reserved for some – the guaranteed, the protected, those who cannot be touched – is denied to the others, the rejects, the exposed, reduced to superfluous, unwelcome bodies who can ultimately be got rid of. Coronavirus has made the immunization of the people within these borders even more exclusive and the exposure of those on the outside even more implacable. The police make this immunopolitics visible in the public space.

The revolt is no accidental response. It would be mistaken to consider it a simple explosion of anger, a directionless reaction against the incumbent suffocation. The scenes that have repeatedly played out in streets and squares, even despite the pandemic, are a direct response to the police's actions – they are a way of taking back the square, restoring the presence of the excluded, and defending the rights of the undesirables.

The close connection between revolt and public space thus again becomes apparent. We find further confirmation of this in the protests that have targeted statues, especially in US cities. Some vilify these protests as iconoclastic riots; and yet, when we look at them more closely, we see that they express the need not only to reoccupy the urban landscape but also to rearticulate its memory. The struggle projects itself onto a past celebrated in monuments to Confederate generals, slave traders, genocidal kings, architects of white supremacy, and propagandists for fascist colonialism. Why go on living in this suffocating atmosphere, surrounded by these statues? If it is wrong to erase the past, it is no less of an error to reify it. Faced with the honours and glory conferred on butchers and oppressors, asserting the perspective of the conquered is an urgent necessity. This gives rise to a clash over rights and memory.

The pandemic has intensified a process that was already under way. It has aggravated an already latent discord between the disciplining of bodies, the militarization of public space, and struggles that express dissent, contradict existing divisions, and undermine the architecture of order. The preventative policing of relations is a regulated 'shielding' measure that culminates in the abolition of contact with the other, who is taken for a possible enemy and source of contagion. This police measure is always already the norm, the marker of immunodemocracy. Thus, the danger of the vibrant, uncontrollable mass, the hazard of the open community, and the spectre of revolt are all kept at bay.

The public space has long been disciplined and controlled. The right to demonstrate can no longer be taken for granted; today, marches, rallies and sit-ins require authorization. If the new revolts are ever more nomadic and transitory, it is no accident that they have taken to any number of sites far beyond the city squares, from the open sea to cross-border spaces and even the decentralized web. Hence the recourse to creative acts and unprecedented means of action. And hence their capacity to reinterpret even biosecurity measures such as antibacterial masks, which are now employed as an outward display of invisibility and openly declared anonymity. The political use of masks sublimates their use as a tool of immunity.

It is, therefore, worth asking whether a politics outside this regimented and surveilled public space is possible. It had become difficult to act in this space even before it was occupied by the sovereign virus. To answer this question, we ought to reconsider the mechanism of public space and turn our gaze to the anarchist extra-politics which is preparing itself through the new revolts.

The Constellation of Revolts

The highly fragmentary character of these revolts is one of their most striking features; it seems difficult even to get an overview of them. While there is no doubt as to their global reach, can we be similarly sure that they are all expressions of the one same phenomenon? Wouldn't it be a bit of an exaggeration to use the same label for such disparate situations? Not least when we consider that, unlike the uprisings of the past, it is not easy to detect any shared aspiration in these revolts. If the insurgents of 1848 set their sights on liberty and the republic, if the revolutionaries of 1917 were guided by the twentieth-century ideal of communism, and if those who took to the streets in the 1960s and 1970s thought that another world was within reach, what unites the revolts of the twenty-first century?

One could emphasize the dissimilarities between these revolts and their discordant means of action and objectives. Some are episodic, others recurrent; some timidly raise their heads, whereas others are openly subversive. But to particularize the revolts, refusing to consider them as articulations of a global movement, amounts to taking the defence of the status quo at face value. It's as if everything was fine – with just a few marginal problems springing up here and there.

When we point to the complicated connections between these revolts – their shifting affinities, their discontinuous movements, their countless correspondences – it may be useful to speak of a 'constellation'. Distant stars in the night sky, scattered sparks that had earlier been hard to make out, suddenly cluster together. In this unprecedented arrangement, even the minor stars take on new value, as their previously hidden correspondence now stands out for all to see. There is no causal nexus, no linear direction, or even the semblance of a beginning. The constellation has no *arché*; anarchic and subversive, it is the fluid outcome of an improvised mobilization that has torn through the homogeneous darkness. In their unexpected harmony, the individual lights grow more intense, lighting each other up, seeming to converge on one focal point. Their conjuncture now appears as an allegorical prefiguration.

Unsurprisingly, Walter Benjamin himself turned to the image of the constellation in his efforts to explode the monumental architectonics of the victors. This is the way to recover what has been erased, discredited, spat upon. That which is not granted historical dignity disrupts the flow of historical becoming. But just as stars die out and sink back into the impenetrable blackness of outer space, revolts, too, can dissolve into the abyss-like backdrop of history. This fiery interruption, almost a simultaneous conflagration, is the here and now of a present that risks escaping us unless it is read in good

9

time. We thus need to keep a nocturnal watch over the sky of history – grasping revolts, calling them back to us and redeeming them with all their charge of disruption and salvation.

Anyone who wants to ascertain the common traits of the contemporary constellation of revolts, without losing sight of their local tendencies, has to accept a twofold challenge. The first lies in seeking out, if not their common thread, at least the string underlying them, bound together by the fact that so many fibres wrap around each other and form a pattern. The second demands attention to the kinetics of revolution, in which revolt occupies an important place but, equally, an enigmatic one.[4]

The official news leaves revolt on the sidelines. If revolt does get past the censor, its power to stir sensation is transformed into spectacle and its transgressive obscurity put on display. It reaches our screens only as far as its gravity, urgency and dimensions warrant. Yet even when the revolt is hyper-visible and overexposed, it is condemned as senseless. There are marches, rallies, mobs in the street and, in a rising crescendo, columns of smoke, broken windows and cars and rubbish bins in flames. Whether in Portland or Baghdad, Athens or Beirut, Hong Kong or Algiers, Santiago or Barcelona, what emerges from the pictures is largely an image of disorder. The confusion of a chaotic, elusive event – that is what these portrayals insist on inferring from this disorder. Hence the lack of reflection on the question of revolt, which nonetheless beats the rhythm of our everyday existence.

If the news paints revolt in obfuscated, sinister colours – whipping up public disdain and fostering interpretative amnesia – this is because revolt extends beyond the logic of institutional politics. To be on the 'outside' is not to be politically irrelevant; this is precisely where revolt's potential force resides, as it attempts to break into public space in order to challenge political governance on its own ground. It should come as no surprise that the version portrayed by the media and institutions relegates revolt to the sidelines, lessens its scope, scrubs it off the agenda and reduces it to nothing more than a spectre. Revolt thus appears as a disturbing shadow which haunts the well-surveilled borders of official current affairs.

For this reason, we need to change our perspective and look at revolt not from the inside – that is, from a stance within the state-centric order – but, rather, from the 'outside' in which it situates itself. Revolt is not a negligible phenomenon, nor is it the residue of the archaic, chaotic, turbulent past that linear progress is supposed to have refined and transcended. It is not anachronistic but anachronic, for it is the result of a different experience of time.

Revolt is a unique dimension of the global disorder – and offers a key to understanding an ever more indecipherable age. The explosions of anger are not lightning that strikes in a clear blue sky but, rather, a symptom, a wake-up call. If revolt is speaking about today, what does it have to say? How can and should it be interpreted? Modernity's criteria no longer seem as valid as they once might have done. Cosmogonies on the meaning of history and totalizing dialectics no longer hold; they overlook the new political antagonisms, which remain unfathomed and impenetrable.

Connected to these questions is the relationship between revolt and politics. Contemporary revolt is generally considered pre-political, if not proto-political, insofar as – partly out of immaturity and partly out of a sort of verbal infantilism – it is unable to formulate authentic demands and hence organize itself into a system of proposals. This would imply that it is unpolitical, if we use this term to refer to its difficulties in entering the institutional political space. But, viewed from the opposite angle, revolt might better be described as hyper-political.

When we look at it more closely, contemporary revolt's relationship with politics is not only a matter of provocation and conflict. The present-day political space is circumscribed by state borders, within which what happens is observed and judged. The modernity of the last two centuries has made the state into the indispensable means and supreme end of all politics. The ruling order is state-centric. The state's undisputed sovereignty remains the criterion that plots the boundaries and draws the map of the present-day geopolitical topography. This has produced a separation between the internal sphere, which is subject to sovereign power, and the external sphere, which is consigned to anarchy. This commonplace dichotomy has introduced a value judgement that distinguishes an inside from an outside, civilization from barbarism, law from lawlessness, order from chaos. State sovereignty has imposed itself as the sole condition of order and the only alternative to anarchy – itself discredited as a simple lack of government, as the confusion that rages on the boundless outside. Yet, globalization has begun to undermine the dichotomy between sovereignty and anarchy, as it exposes all the limits of a politics anchored in traditional borders. If the state remains the epicentre of the new global disorder, the landscape on the other side of the border is now being populated by different protagonists. New phenomena such as migration are tearing open a gap that affords a glimpse of what is happening outside – obliging us to leave behind this dichotomy and embrace a new perspective.

Likewise, revolt is situated outside of sovereignty, in the open ground that has always been the province of anarchy. This ground should be seen not only as a space between one border and another but also as a fissure, a small opening into the internal landscape. Revolt shows the state as it is seen from the windows of the peripheral neighbourhoods, through the eyes of those who are left out or ruled out. It is obvious why, helped by the media narrative, state politics should seek to make revolt obscure and marginal. For what is at stake is not merely – or not so much – some single demand or contingent grievance.

Revolt ultimately puts the state itself into question. Whether the state is democratic or despotic, secular or religious, revolt shines a light on its violence and strips it of its sovereignty. A characteristic of the revolts of the present era – which, not by accident, first began with the slogan '¡Que se vayan todos, que no quede ninguno!' – is this separation between power and people. Despite the state's effort to legitimize itself – often by spreading alarm and flaunting its own self-confidence – this separation would now appear to be a definitive fracture. The sovereign and authoritarian reaction, itself the product of a sovereignty that has been bled dry, cannot do anything to alter this process.

In the streets and squares, political governance – an abstract administrative exercise – vaunts its inquisitorial aspect in its bid to confront a mass which it has proven unable to govern. The ungoverned burst on the scene, making their appearance in order to decry the unrepresentativeness of political institutions. This points not only to the crisis of representation, which populism so exploits, but also to a redefinition of the political space itself. The heterogeneous forms and modalities of this conflict pervade and upset the global landscape. This explains why revolt is so eminently political.

Individual demands and contingent motives are unable to offer an exhaustive explanation of this phenomenon. The killing of a demonstrator, a law that restricts democratic freedoms, an unpunished rape, a fuel price hike, a sudden increase in metro fares, the latest corruption scandal, the transformation of a park into a shopping centre, a pension reform, a religious fundamentalist reprisal – these particular causes are all necessary to any analysis of this phenomenon. Yet they are not enough to understand its full complexity. The factors behind any revolt can never be reduced to any single cause. They all originate from a combination and intertwining of different motives, which are not just economic in character but also political and existential.

Revolt expresses an unspecific malaise, demonstrates a vague but nagging unease, and reveals all the expectations that have been disappointed. The world we have before us is quite different from the development that was promised and all the boasts of progress. For this is a world that allows and fosters yawning inequalities, the logic of profit, the plundering of the future, and the spectacular arrogance of a few faced with the impotence of the many.

Between Politics and Police

A revolt's political potential is realized when it manages to highlight injustice within the surveilled confines of the public space and, in so doing, reconfigures this space itself. That is why revolt is above all a practice of irruption – arriving from the margins, it embarrasses government policy and brings its policing function out into the open. This elision is no accident. The etymological link between 'policy' and 'police' ought to be taken seriously. We can continue along the path that Jacques Rancière indicated as he looked beyond the restrictive meaning usually attributed to the term 'police'.[5] Policing is not simply a matter of truncheons, armoured cars and interrogation rooms, or even just of the state's repressive apparatus. The so-called public order which the police manage stretches far wider than this apparatus – and, for this reason, the police's role is decisive, even if it is not always obvious. The police discipline bodies, by allowing them to meet or by banning them from assembling, and also structure space itself, assigning roles, establishing prerogatives and competences – to have, to do, to say. They determine who can occupy what post and regulate the faculty of appearance. But, above all, they govern order – the order of the visible and the speakable, fixing the limits of participation. They include and exclude, discriminating between who does and doesn't have a share.

Usually, a perspective internal to governance is taken for granted. Thus, beyond the administration of public order, politics vanishes and is reduced to policing alone. Indeed, this is what remains of a politics caught in the pincers of economics and crushed under a well-armoured bureaucratic machinery. This politics ends up as a mere residue, an eloquent reminder of its own tragic absence. But politics cannot be limited to the walls of the *pólis* alone – especially if that is taken to mean the perimeter of the state. This is especially true in the complex, unstable, fragmentary landscape of the new millennium. Whoever wears the blinkers of governance will be unable to explain the instabilities and tensions within these walls, or still less the movements that agitate the space beyond the borders, vilified as mere chaos and confusion. Everything that comes from the 'outside' appears as a spectre: it is both an illusory shadow and an imminent threat. Just as migration is turned into a matter of clandestine intrigues, revolt is cast as dark, apolitical disorder. A normative, governmental approach cannot do otherwise.

Only a politics that takes the opposite approach – one which moves from the edges, breaks down the barriers, and refuses any policing function – can redeem the name of politics. Such a politics is present wherever conflicts explode, wherever struggles break out. It makes injustice a shared problem for all; it puts dissent on display, sheds light on the invisible and the vilified, defends those with nothing to defend, contradicts the present divisions and shows the contingency of order. It breaks the policing hierarchy of *arché*, which claims a monopoly on principle and purports to have established its own command. There is no politics, if not in the anarchic interruption, in the breach where, as soon as the call for equality can make itself audible, it contradicts the governmental logic. This breach is the space where the being-together of the community is constantly rebuilt anew.

Occupations: From the Factories to the Squares

Although spontaneous movements come and go, the forms of protest that have studded the global landscape in recent decades do display novel and peculiar characteristics.

Place de la République, Taksim Square, Liberty Plaza, Puerta del Sol – there have been countless occupations in public squares across continents. People take to the streets, coming together in some nerve-centre of the city which has been chosen for their assembly. It is as if their main concern was to avoid dispersal, to gather in a common space and at a common time despite their diverse provenance. The squares which they occupy are, in general, devoted to the circulation of traffic or simply to pedestrians or those at a loose end. The demonstrators stop there for hours, days, nights: they leave and come back again. It is almost as if they represent an alternative community.

But why occupy squares, specifically? Why not factories, or even universities – where occupations were commonplace even just a few years ago, but are now increasingly rare?

This turn from the factory to the public square ought not to be seen as a mere twist of fate, a trivial question of the logistics of protest. The idea that has inspired and oriented the workers' movement throughout its momentous history holds that labour constitutes a world in common, even if it is alienated in market relations and vampirized in state structures. It is a community because of its horizontal structure and its place within a system of production and exchange which could keep going even without hierarchies, bosses and owners. This movement's vision of the future held that the relations mediated by the abstraction of money and the commodity would eventually be overcome, as the relations between producers were redeemed and finally made human. Such a vision underpinned and fed the development of the various currents of trade unionism, socialism and anarchism. Hence the conception and the modality of a struggle understood as the final seizure of power by the collective worker.

Something similar can be said of the school and university occupations that punctuated the various phases of the student movement, in its different forms, from the 1960s onwards, peaking in the 1970s. These occupations were also coloured by a deep-seated, robust conviction that the world to come was already within reach – only a night of waiting away.

This fervour, this nervous expectation, this hope, has now all but vanished. The sentiments and the aspirations that pervade and agitate the squares today are rather more mixed, more complex, more contradictory. Occupations have left the factories and workplaces behind and largely also the universities, schools, and all the sites where social functions are performed – so many strategic hubs where it had once been possible for forces in conflict to come together. This turn has a clear political significance: it amounts to a recognition that, in the age of advanced capitalism, global debt, outsourced industries and growing precarity, labour no longer constitutes a community. Or, better, work is just the way in which each person involved in a merciless competition manages their own 'human capital'. Moreover, as biopolitics teaches, today the whole of human life, and not just labour power alone, is summoned into use and cannibalized. This marks a decisive difference from the protests of the past and from such traditional forms of struggle as the strike.

Community can no longer be presupposed, only aspired to and sought out with great difficulty. Now that workplaces have been cast out of the topography of visibility, community has to be staged elsewhere; it has to be represented at some distance from the great palaces earmarked as the sites of representation. This also helps to explain the role of the assembly, where the other people – that is, the unrepresented people – must find their place. The new assemblies are attempts at community. Yet the aspiration that guides them seems to go no further than the gratification of being together.

The gathering plays out in the square, a space left empty by politics. It is, at the same time, a symbolic reference to the *agorá*, the first site of democracy and the last reserve available to community. This helps explain the mixing of resignation and resistance that takes place there. Being together means reacting against a world that isolates and separates. This is an ethical as well as a political response. In this sense, the occupation itself is already opposition. In the square, different forms of mobilization converge, from feminists to human rights activists, from environmentalists to the defenders of migrants, and from pacifists to antiracists. Nonetheless, this convergence is often only a temporary adding together of single struggles, and they do not manage to establish connections with one another.

With party slogans no longer able to appeal to the masses, the square is the theatre of invention – comics and actors are thus often present. Here, new gestures are devised, unprecedented and spectacular actions are experimented with, creative slogans are launched, and irreverent wordplay appears on placards and banners. But when the final notes of the collective chant of resistance die out, from one square to another the only apparent echo is the sharp 'no' of a global refusal of the global world.

An assertion of democracy and a practical show of solidarity, the squares movement risks dissipating amidst myriad particular struggles – or even being reintegrated by the agenda of official politics. It does not exert lasting influence, does not go beyond dissent, does not seem to leave a mark on the partition of the city which – as was apparent already in Plato's studies – turns out to be justice itself. When workers went on strike, this did not involve only an occupation of the factories but also a subversion and redistribution of spaces. But, while the squares movement tries to react against the dispersion brought by capitalism, it does not manage to reconfigure the public space.

Bella ciao: Notes of Resistance

Bella ciao reverberates through the streets of Beirut. Its beat follows the determined rhythm set by the Kurdish women fighting in Rojava. It is carried by the fierce wind of revolt through the cities of Chile. It thunders through a Barcelona airport occupied by pro-independence activists. It is the accompaniment to the Fridays for Future protests. And it also makes its return to the Italian city squares – where it had in fact never been forgotten – pushing back the black wave of racist sovereignty. But even its most recent past has the richest of histories. How can anyone forget the collective chorus which raised its voice in Gezi Park? Or the version which the Nuit Debout orchestra played in Place de la République, in its homage to the demonstrators fighting against labour-market reforms?

A stateless anthem that can claim no fatherland or parentage, *Bella ciao* is the result of surprising combinations and unusual cross-contaminations. Ancient texts by Provençal troubadours enter into harmony with a klezmer melody; it became the ballad of Italian rice-cleaning women and, at the end of the war, the song of the partisans. By its very nature, *Bella ciao* is international in inspiration. It offers a wake-up call, and also a call to arms, sounding the alarm at the invader's coming victory and insisting on the urgent need for a response. In the background stands the dark shadow of fascism. The flower on the grave is the tribute paid by those who bear the memory of the fallen partisan and will continue along the same path. Unsurprisingly, given *Bella ciao*'s capacity to inflame people's souls and mobilize them in a shared opposition, it has transcended borders, rising up as a paean to struggle in the globalized world.[6] It provides not just a hymn to freedom but notes of resistance. And these notes ring out every time that the situation becomes unbearable, indignation grows, and danger mounts.

This resistance is a matter not of obeying some external obligation but of responding to a vital necessity. Those who resist have not surrendered, have not succumbed to resignation; rather, they respond and defend themselves. So, even if resistance comes afterwards – as a consequence – this does not mean that it is subordinate. The balance of forces is asymmetrical, the conditions unfavourable. The adversary is irresistibly stronger; history seems to be on his side. Those summoned to resist are those who, even as they are about to succumb, will not allow their weakness to reduce them to impotence. They will not let today's defeat translate into capitulation or permit a temporary outcome to be read as the oracle of destiny.

The partisan keeps her eyes down, but her head does not fall. Rather, she becomes more vigilant, almost suspicious. The partisan does not desist or succumb to resignation but says – 'enough'. She proclaims this quietly, not triumphantly. Yet the signal is clear. Resistance is an unyielding principle.

But what follows from this point of principle is not a straight line. Likewise, the confrontation is never frontal, unless this should become unavoidable. The paths of resistance are tortuous, bending, transversal – and this, not out of vacillation or hesitation but in order to get around obstacles, to avoid ambushes and hidden threats. Resistance is a movement without the verticality of the uprising or the open face of rebellion; rather, it has the diffuse, anonymous latency of clandestinity. The partisan looks for cover, digs tunnels, delves into crypts and catacombs. She is a refugee in the underground, from where she undermines the dominant edifice and from where all kinds of subversion are prepared. She is kept going by her stubborn patience, her subterranean energy, the obstinate watchfulness of a hope that never surrenders.

Resistance is an oblique, transversal tactic: it moves along the sidelines and works in the margins. The partisan does not confront the enemy for the sake of inflicting a defeat on him; rather, she defends herself from the adversary in order to force him to release his grip. She disarms him with her own arms, subverts his rules, wrong-foots and disorients him. She thus tries to gain ever more space and time for herself, and for reorganization. The only victory that she seeks is liberation itself.

While resistance is specific and of its moment, it bets on a longer-term future. It is reactive but not subaltern to the force it is resisting. It does not propose alternatives but opens up possibilities, whose contours remain unknown. Its fixed principle is a foundational limit that points to a beyond, reveals an outside. Better, there are multiple points of resistance; but they risk being so tiny as to disappear without a trace. Not by chance, the protagonists are often anonymous, their actions unknown. But precisely in this filigree of resistance it becomes clear that another world is possible. In this sense, resistance already goes beyond mere indignation, simple refusal: it has a disobedient heart, the prelude to revolt.

The partisan has often been considered an 'irregular' combatant. This is owing to her transversality, which situates her on the margins, outside the domain of right. Thus according to Carl Schmitt, the partisan – this unprecedented figure in the political landscape – undermines the classic war between states; for the partisan fights in illegality.[7] To tell the truth, the partisan's battle is not military but political in character. As the name suggests, the partisan's sympathies lie with a given side, and she espouses a certain cause. Her struggle is shaped by a political commitment. In the name of the struggle which she considers legitimate, she may even lay claim to a legality other than that of the sovereign powers against whom she is fighting. This is what happened in the wars of liberation. Hence the opposing perspectives on the partisans: one side takes them for 'bandits' but, as we read on so many plaques around Italy, the other sees them as 'fallen for freedom'. Despite the attempts to legalize the partisan, absorbing them into juridical normality without compromising the law itself, there remains this fissure, an open laceration through which other more disruptive figures make their entrance onto the world stage.

The partisan is, moreover, always the symbol of an irregularity which asserts its own legitimacy within the political environment limited by state borders. This shows why resistance, with the responses it has to offer, is such a resource for political invention.

In the contemporary world, starting in the liberal democracies, politics has lost so much of its value that it is no longer seen as a constitutive element of human existence. Disaffection, abstention and lack of interest in current affairs are but hints that point to a deeper phenomenon – the fact that political existence is no longer a destiny, in the sense that existence is no longer destined for the *pólis*. Self-defence and the protection of one's own living being – or better, immunization – count for rather more. Politics becomes a vital need only in a negative sense, when we become aware of some threat. Each looks out for his own and seeks to preserve himself.

Resistance could be seen as the other face of immunization. But, while it starts out from a similar defensive need, it heads along different paths. Those who self-immunize, protecting themselves from the risk of contact and exposure to the other, turn in on themselves within an immunitarian fortress – the most restrictive possible, held together by fear. The partisan keeps her eyes down but steps up her vigilance, and is thus able to see transversal paths different from a governing order whose legitimacy has collapsed. Her rebellious energy is contagious, her disposition shared. The partisan's front line unites forces, experiences and different ideas, though these may head off in different directions again once adversity has been overcome. In this lie both the value of resistance and its limits.

A Spectral Era

Wherever the wind of resistance blows, the spirit of revolt flutters. But who can really know what is being prepared in the passageways, in the arcades, in the underpasses? Not even the apparent eclipse of events could lead us to the conclusion that the quiet stirrings of resistance have ceased altogether. Politics is not limited to the exceptional event – and one ought not underestimate, still less ignore, the latent tension that precedes the event, as its future perfect. So, we need to keep our eyes peeled and our ears close to the ground, in order to sense the imperceptible rumblings of history and observe its barely noticed tremors.

At this point, it is hard to avoid our thoughts turning to the old mole. Inspired by Hegel and Shakespeare, Marx adopted the mole as a symbol of revolution after he had seen a series of searing defeats. Short-sighted and fragile, patient and stubborn, in its continual coming and goings the mole turns back and forth again, inadvertently returning to the point from which it started out, then tirelessly setting off again. As it digs down further, it sometimes becomes invisible, but it never disappears. And, down underground, the mole's amiable bustling opens the way to new breakthroughs. Revolutions may fail or be betrayed, but they are not easily erased from the memory of the defeated; they turn into a diffuse dissent, continue in invasive absences, transform into spectral presences. The revolution, as Derrida showed, is a question of moles and spectres, troubling visions and promising apparitions.[8] It all began with a spectre haunting Europe that ended up haunting the whole world. But the ambivalence of this spectre is well known: no one knows if we are dealing with the return of a phantom from the past or else the appearance of a spirit of the future. Or both. Perhaps it is the final death rattle of a ghost now in its twilight, or perhaps a gust of wind that is still too slight and airy.

It is almost impossible to avoid confusing spectre and spirit – especially so in a spectral era such as this one, in which the spirit seems to withdraw and make way for a diffuse frenzy, a convulsive agitation. The new world disorder lends itself to all sorts of apparitions: snake-oil sellers, illusion merchants, ludicrous charlatans and shadowy conspiracy theorists. Amidst the hidden ferments, nocturnal conventicles and explosions of rage, deciphering the space of politics seems like a formidable task.

In a 2015 article tellingly entitled 'Why Revolution is No Longer Possible', Byung-Chul Han builds on the debate he had with Antonio Negri in a Berlin theatre.[9] As against Negri's optimistic perspective and 'overly naïve' hope in the Multitude rising up against Empire, Han replied by emphasizing the stability of the neoliberal system, which is 'not repressive but seductive'. For this very reason, it is able to neutralize the evanescent resistance that does survive. Every class struggle mutates into a conflict within the individual, who blames not society but rather herself. This is how this system constantly immunizes itself. Individuals, who are always already defeated and isolated, set against each other by merciless competition, do not solidarize or unite with one another in a multitude or rise up in mass revolution or global protest.

This – so to speak, internal – line of approach shrewdly analyses the self-perpetuation of power and its ability to ward off any potential challengers. It portrays domination as a well-oiled machine, a system that neatly fits together, almost a technological device. But while politics is profoundly conditioned by technology, it is not itself technology. Cracks, rifts and dissonances emerge all over the place. Without doubt, no one today can imagine themselves standing in direct confrontation with capitalism, simply because capitalism is the world itself – a world in which the centre is both everywhere and nowhere. Capitalist logic permeates body and soul, saturates the environment, leaves its mark on the forms of life. But if such a frontal clash appears antiquated, that does not deny that margins of dissent may gradually arise. We need to change our perspective and look more from the outside, from around the edges of politics. This will allow us to make out the spaces of resistance, the squares where solidarity is put on display and the desire for community articulated. Between the temptation of over-triumphalist hypotheses and gloomily defeatist diagnoses, there is perhaps a different way of looking at the myriad different struggles across the planet that put the traditional schemas into question and reconfigure public space.

In Search of the Lost Revolution

Since the end of the twentieth century, 'revolution' has been the name for an event that did not happen or, worse, an event which appeared in the trappings of its absolute denial. Across the history of whole generations this event had been the object of feverish expectations, but now it seemed that not even its name could survive. For it was now disfigured by its totalitarian caricature, passed off as the archaic remnant of a past now to be forgotten, stigmatized as the emblem of subversive intrigues that ought to be repudiated. Revolution is a name erased from public memory and denigrated in liberal democracy's normative discourse.

Yet in this there was not only censure but also a certain self-censure. In his book *Left-Wing Melancholia: Marxism, History, and Memory*, Enzo Traverso reconstructs the effects of a loss which seemed irreparable and a grief that is impossible to process.[10] The whole history of revolutionary movements has been patterned by defeats. The heroic testimonies to the Paris Commune, the dramatic accounts of the Spartacist uprising, the sorrowful images of Spanish Republican exiles, and the striking photo – itself a kind of war trophy – immortalizing Che Guevara's corpse, each stirred indignation and admiration, regret and courage, but never brought impotence and dejection. Grief was a ritual passage in a hope which, starting from a critical vision of the past, stretched out to the future. This hope now itself seemed to dissipate, buried under the rubble of the Berlin Wall and crushed by the weight of an epochal failure.

Even before it could be censured, grief proved impossible. How could one process the disappearance of something which had never even taken place? Unless, that is, one took the nightmare for the dream, confusing the revolution with its perverse metamorphosis, reducing communism to its totalitarian version and being forced to recognize oneself in the mirror of state Stalinism. Such an identification was unacceptable – and thus grief was inhibited. So, what defeat was there to lament? What loss was there to process? The loss of a defeated, subdued, destroyed revolution? Or that of a revolution that had gone astray, abandoned and drifting beyond reach? Loss assumed the sense not so much of a defeat as of an absence. This is what the search for the lost revolution would suggest, in all its ambivalence. Retracing the itinerary set out by Proust, this meant, after an initial estrangement, the rediscovery of repressed potentials and the liberation of broken promises.[11]

One could simply have turned one's back on that heap of irrecoverable ruins, so difficult to clear away and still more so to rebuild. This was all that seemed to remain of centuries of struggles after the collapse in 1989 – the date that condensed a historic turning point, a watershed moment that heralded the age of liberal order. Or so it would have done, except that the collapse – in which the last generation of lost revolts, in the 1960s and 1970s, also crumbled – also took down all utopias with it. The time that imposed itself with this collapse was the time of a future displaced into a past of renunciation, resignation and retreat. In the long run, social democracy would not be left undamaged either; ever prone to compromise and accommodation, as it became fully assimilated it gradually disappeared.

This searching for the lost revolution indicates the impossibility of a satisfactory grieving process such as could lead to acceptance of a present order devoid of alternatives. At the same time, it implies the recovery of one of the left's hidden traditions – its tradition of melancholia. This latter was overlooked or passed over in silence in the official propaganda discourse; it was overshadowed by the canonical representations of a magnificent future with its glorious epic and its ineluctable progress. Yet melancholia continued as a discreet, almost intangible underground stream, before ultimately resurfacing among the ruins of the late twentieth century. It refutes the old progressive teleological vision which sees socialism as the end of history. Melancholia emerges from the shipwreck of this naive and arrogant certainty. If grief is a transition – and thus has an end – melancholia is an enduring, incomplete disposition. Without regressing into a conservative passivity and regret for what once was, melancholia projects itself through the traumas of defeat into nostalgia for what was long awaited but never came. It thus revives the memory of promise.

Just a few months separated the fall of the Berlin Wall from the fiftieth anniversary of the death of Walter Benjamin. Fleeing the Nazis, on 26 September 1940 he committed suicide in Portbou, a Catalan village backing on to the French border. Half a century later, 1990 saw the commemoration of a philosopher who had long remained on the margins of European culture, that German Jew who had offered a unique conjugation of Marxism and messianism. This was no accident. Benjamin's angel, with its eyes wide open and its gaze fixed on the ruins, arrived at just the right moment – to recognize progress as a dangerous, paralysing myth, but also to allude to the possibility of a messianic brake, the chance of revolution contained in each moment. Not everything was definitively lost. The Parisian *Arcades* and especially the *Theses on the Concept of History* soon became the texts of reference for those on the left who did not let themselves be led astray by the sirens of anti-totalitarianism or, still less, of liberalism. What is more, these texts were a resource for radically rethinking the left, providing the means by which to resist the reactionary wave. In the moment of danger, the past could illuminate the future. This was what Benjamin taught, as a melancholic, messianic watchman whose writings provided bearings amidst the storm of capitalism and its emptied out time.

What Does Revolt Mean?

The word 'revolt' brings to mind the upheavals in the Italian cities of the Renaissance, the civil strife that raged both within and outside their walls, and the riots and uprisings that ultimately led Machiavelli to introduce into his theory the term *status* – the state. By this, Machiavelli meant that form of firm, stable, unchanging government that would subsequently posit itself as the only possible one. Indeed, this was precisely the scenario in which the Italian word *rivolta* – now detached from the verb *rivolgere* (turn, address) and thus from the Latin *revolvere* (retreat, turn back) – entered the political arena, assuming an increasingly metaphorical value. It alludes to an upheaval, a change – thus revealing a link with revolution which was not limited to etymology alone. But already centuries before revolution, revolt expressed the rejection of authority. The verb 'revolt' alluded to a volte-face: it meant changing sides, breaking with obedience, escaping command. Accounts from the time emphasize this point and tell of the rebels and the disobedient in cities across the Italian peninsula. From the outset, revolt was inspired with a certain breath of anarchy – a factor which ought not be forgotten when we look at the contemporary landscape.

The Italian word emigrated into various languages – from French to German, English and Spanish. It brought with it the winds of sedition, but it also adapted to the new circumstances. It thus increasingly appeared together with an 'against' which altered its character and strongly emphasized its oppositional character. Proceeding along these passageways – and especially within the French context – it gradually took on moral and psychological traits, even without losing its political value. One could thus speak of revolt also as a description of individual indignation.

We cannot neglect one famous episode here. On the night of 14 July 1789, Louis XVI learned from the duc de la Rochefoucauld-Liancourt about the storming of the Bastille: some of the prisoners had been freed and the royal troops had deserted their posts, faced with the popular assault. This led to all manner of disorder. 'Is this a revolt?' the king asked. 'No, sire, it is a revolution', the duke replied. The term 'revolution' appeared on the political stage for the first time: having previously designated a circular movement in the skies, it transferred down to earth to become the name for a new type of irresistible movement. Over the centuries to come, this term would orient forces and draw battle lines. The assault on the Bastille was not a revolt but a revolution. The change could not be stopped. The duke's unexpected reply was thus, so to speak, the birth certificate of revolution. The king asked around, seeking information that would help him evaluate what means were needed to confront this challenge. But what had happened had the mark of the irrevocable. The decisive moment had already sounded. The gates of history had opened up forever to the multitude bursting through the streets of the city, to the poor and oppressed who, for centuries relegated to humiliation and gloomy, narrow horizons, finally came out into the open to become free protagonists of their own lives.

Revolution thus made its first appearance accompanied by revolt. But while the duke's reply, correcting the king's own reaction, marked a watershed moment, it also seemed to put revolt in the shadows, all but negating it. It is as if the two terms were antinomic; as for the revolution, to be recognized it had first to be counterposed to revolt.

Such an antinomic vision ended up prevailing more or less everywhere – in political thought as in philosophy and literature. This schema was reproduced in many variants, but fundamentally all of them proposed a clear antithesis. It is as if these two poles were so opposed in tendency that each excluded the other. If there is revolution, there is no revolt – and vice versa. Rarely is the emphasis placed on the transition between the two; more often it is implied that there is a divergence or a yawning abyss between them.

Revolt ends up the worse for this – for it represents the negative pole of this equation. Accused of lacking a (sufficiently) political character, revolt appears as the obscure, mute chaos, that terrifying disorder that loomed already among the slaves on the borders of the *pólis*. In this portrayal, revolt is presented as subject to the diktats of an immediate *pathos* and incapable of raising the standard of liberty or of openly challenging sovereign power. This was also the way in which Hannah Arendt spoke of revolt. She projected revolt into the past and separated it from revolution – characterizing this latter as the true beginning that demanded legitimacy as it forcefully made its way into the public space.[12]

All too spontaneous, impatient and impetuous, revolt is mostly considered the result of a whim, an unstable temperament, an uncontrollable passion – setting it at a distance from reason, careful observation and strategic decision-making. It seethes with grievance, it explodes with rage; but, in the end, all that remains of this destructive fury are miserable wreckage and useless fragments. It is tormented by desperation, sometimes to the dizzying point of sacrifice – with no other effect than the loss of one's own life, as in the countless forgotten rebellions mounted by African-American slaves.

Revolt is considered short-sighted – blind, even. Indifferent to history, whose course it is supposedly unable to impact, it is accused of rising up only out of a sharp refusal of today, without ever raising its sights towards tomorrow. This supposedly condemns it to futurelessness. But it is also said to have a restricted perspective on space, unable to see beyond the enemy to be fought and the miseries to be overcome. In this reading, it remains disoriented in its own native surroundings, unable to seal alliances or connect with other struggles, whether nearby or far away.

In this understanding, even victorious revolts do not seal any triumph: they lead nowhere and have no future. They could do no more than destroy power without taking power. This is the perennial dilemma of the great leaders of revolts: Spartacus, Thomas Müntzer and Pancho Villa. Despite the great distance between these figures, they have in common the fact that they each mounted an explosive adventure in revolt against injustice. Even when Pancho Villa seemed to have established himself in power, he was unwilling or unable to govern; he did not administer, did not organize, did not decide. Paradoxically, revolt comes to a stop the very instant that it risks success, in the moment that it has the opportunity to change history. The most emblematic example of this is Spartacus, who stopped his advance before a now defenceless Rome. There was nothing left but to march into the city – but Spartacus refused to do this. Was this not the disorientation of a man in revolt who was not yet a revolutionary? Was this not the perplexity of an ex-slave who wouldn't know what to do with Rome? In any case, he resumed his journey, set off marching towards the mountains again – and left the burden of his triumph behind. Many thus conclude that his endeavours left Roman society intact without bringing any new beginning. But is that really the case?

As far as power is concerned, revolt can be considered nomadic. It can surge dizzyingly through the city with its electric charge, its burning flame, its destructive potential, its errant force, and can even escape again in the end. But it remains a nomad, camping in the tents on the periphery among the migrants, the stateless, the homeless, the bandits and the vagabonds. Unlike the revolution, which tries to conquer the headquarters and establish itself therein, the revolt does not settle, is not sedentary. In short: while the revolt limits itself to tearing down power, the revolution tries to institution-alize itself.

Success or failure does not make the difference. The scale of a revolt, or even its victory, does not change its significance – it is neither a small revolution nor, still less, a failed one. The divergence is reiterated, and the gap appears impossible to overcome. Lacking leadership, in the sense of either a vanguard or a command, a revolt does not know how to govern. This is true right from the beginning of the revolt – and is there even a beginning? It expresses only the impos-sibility of living. It externalizes the existential malaise that cannot be processed other than in a silent refusal or in a cry which is unable to find a verbal, political form. That is why revolt conserves an individual stamp and no community can take form.

The negative judgements on revolt continue. The revolt has no doctrine, no project, no programme. If it does have some insight, the flicker of a thought, this is merely accidental. It does not begin, like the revolution, with an idea that is to be realized in history, following specific tracks from which one must not diverge. Revolution rhymes with evolution. Revolt, however, does not join in the great march of progress and is not part of the plan for emancipation. Rather, it is a fracture, an interruption, the second in which the train derails. Revolt is not progressive – there is no guarantee that it will not turn out to be reactionary. In its headlong rush, it could even take the unpredictable direction of the past it has just refused. Not to mention that – as some sarcastic commentators suggest – it could even be good news for the government in power. Even if it is hardly shaken, it could still take the revolt as an opportunity to firm up its own apparatus, put the army to the test and lubricate the already well-oiled policing machine.

As well as lacking a beginning, the revolt is simultaneously said to be destined to leave no effect. It would, on this reading, dissipate just as rapidly as it emerged, leaving no trace other than a tragic defeat. Countless revolts thus remain condemned to silence and oblivion, at the seabed of human history.

The Individual's Cry – and the Wounds of History

Based on a strong, blunt, rigid dichotomy, this vision definitively condemns revolt in the name of the revolution. This vision is also near ubiquitous; it is shared, for example, even by a great writer such as Victor Hugo, who offered such an unforgettable description of revolt in his *Les Misérables*. But even Marx and Engels much preferred evolutionary, homogeneous, persistent change to rash actions. This explains why Marx overlooked anticolonial uprisings – which anarchists, however, supported – and why, failing to attribute sufficient weight to the abolition of slavery, he ended up underestimating the Haitian Revolution led by the 'Black Jacobins'. One might think of this in terms of the usual disagreements between anarchists and Marxists. But even Bakunin's famous pages in defence of revolt do not offer any radically different perspective. Considering it 'elemental, chaotic, and merciless in nature', as per certain recurrent stereotypes, his positive appreciation of revolt above owed to its 'negative' side its 'real passion for destruction'. Like it or not, Bakunin argues, 'there can be no revolution without widespread and passionate destruction.' But for him, too, while revolt is indispensable, it can never 'achiev[e] the ultimate aims of the revolutionary cause'.[13]

43

In the mid-twentieth century, inspired by the news coming from the Soviet revolution, revolt found its champion in Albert Camus. The term took on philosophical importance: *L'Homme révolté* (*The Rebel: An Essay on Man in Revolt*) came out on 18 October 1951, immediately prompting controversy. Openly challenged, the book became a target for many intellectuals close to Sartre. The theme of the debate, which gradually took on more bitter and personal tones, was the relationship between violence and politics. 'Does the end justify the means? That is possible', Camus observed close to the end of his book. 'But what will justify the end?'[14] The question he posed reflected the rather troubling results of actually existing communism. But it would be rash, indeed misleading, to see this polemic, which led to Camus's definitive break with Sartre, as a clash between Marxist orthodoxy and libertarian thought; their positions were much more composite and indefinite than that.

Camus sought to provide a balance-sheet of the twentieth-century revolutions inspired by Marx in light of the revelations on their labour camps, their trials against dissidents, and their repressive techniques. He pointed an accusing finger against totalitarianism, with a timbre and modalities similar to Arendt's own. But the balance-sheet he drew was less a considered survey than a settling of accounts. Marx was to pay the price – not only was he called into the dock alongside Lenin,

Trotsky and Stalin, but he was even considered the ideologue truly at fault for the totalitarian turn. In this summary judgement, we can make out a political ambiguity for which Camus would long be criticized. He spoke of his almost visceral intolerance for injustice, though he did not explain so much as reference why he was on the side of the downtrodden. His hatchet crashed down on the revolution itself, always and everywhere guilty of seeking to introduce the ideal into history, taking advantage of the revolt which it then systematically ended up betraying, terrorizing and butchering. The surprising thing, in his gloomy discourse on revolution and its inevitable failure, is the clear antithesis it establishes between revolution and revolt. Camus rules out the possibility of a passageway, a continuity, between the two: one could be a man in revolt or else a revolutionary.[15] Moreover, the revolutionary's fate was set in advance: either he would become an oppressor or end up as a heretic. But, in so doing, Camus did no more than adopt the clichéd understanding of the relationship between revolt and revolution, then turn it on its head. Hence his intense – and, in parts, heart-rending – tribute to revolt, alas one that also bore unmistakeable moralistic notes, as underlined by Sartre.[16]

The revolt is the cry of the individual rebelling against the absurdity of existence, her refusal of injustice, her bid to repel the horrors. Behind the slave's 'volte-face', rejecting the master's command, we can make out the resistance of the individual who refuses to be ground down by the new totalitarian power's bureaucratic machine. The revolt sets down a limit; and, even as it says 'no', it also says 'yes'. The man in revolt pushes back against intrusion but also stands steadfast by that within himself which he must preserve, starting with his own freedom. In this sense, revolt is an indelible dimension of existence. The estranged individual, feeling alien to this world, rebels. But this estrangement is the very thing that he shares with others, which makes him feel that they are in the same boat. 'I revolt – therefore we exist.'[17]

Showing, among other things, his loyalty to the Spanish cause, in 1936 Camus had contributed to the production of the play *Revolt in Asturias*. It tells the story of the Oviedo miners' uprising, which was bloodily suppressed by the Guardia Civil. In this story, the individual carries the charge of libertarian energy with his quixotic gesture; and, similarly, the protagonist of the revolt is always the individual, in his profound moral indignation, without this thereby creating any opening to collective action.

Camus could thus boast the undoubted merit of having elevated revolt to a theme of literary reflection, although without this having political consequences. Revolt is short-term and has no lasting effects; it bears no impact on ways of seeing revolution. And the dilemma still remains: if the revolt is pure and intractable, it renounces power and condemns itself to impotence; but whenever it does deal with power, it is immediately already subdued.[18]

So, even those who seemingly want to defend revolt end up demoting it into the desolate recesses of history and relegating it to the margins of politics. But does the antithesis between revolt and revolution really bear scrutiny? Can this conceptual dichotomy be taken for granted? Perhaps they are both part of a revolutionary kinetics in which it is impossible to define where the one flows into the other. Would that not suggest that it is also time to rethink revolution itself? And to say that revolt leaves no effects would be to underestimate the importance of testimony; this would mean understanding history in a static manner as if the past were closed and concluded forever and could not be read with a different key in a different present. The revolt in the Warsaw ghetto, which took place when all was lost, was not a gesture of desperation or an act of pride but an unforgettable appeal from the past inscribed in the history of the defeated, a call awaiting its redemption.

Perhaps only a philosopher prepared to base progress on the idea of catastrophe, inclined to break open the dialectic and make out the fractures and discontinuities within history's apparently straight path forward – a philosopher ready to challenge Marx's legendary locomotive with the no less effective image of the emergency brake – could have radically rethought the revolution. For Benjamin, the laceration that suddenly opens up, from which emerge the unhealed wounds of history, sounds the long-awaited explosion, the moment of legitimate revolutionary violence. Here, revolution is a political event with messianic notes. It is no surprise that, influenced by anarchism, Benjamin should have looked to the explosive charge, to ecstatic intoxication. This dovetails with the figure of the intellectual who, like a rag-picker, haunts the passages and the subways of Paris to pick up the murmuring and the rustling of the forgotten, the banished and the marginalized. But on only a couple of occasions does Benjamin's revolution touch upon revolt. The first is in 1926, during his 'tour of German inflation', where he pauses to talk about poverty. Here, the spark to revolt is not the torment experienced by an individual but, rather, the poverty of others. No one has any right to make peace with this 'gigantic shadow' faced with which one should take not 'the downhill road of grief, but the rising path of revolt'.[19] Three years later, citing Bakunin, Benjamin asked if it is possible to maintain the 'element of intoxication' at work within every revolutionary act, its 'anarchic' element – that is, conjugating revolt with revolution in order to make this latter 'a praxis oscillating between fitness exercises and celebration in advance'.[20]

Benjamin says nothing further – and his question remains unanswered. Herbert Marcuse would almost explicitly pick up on this same problem. An eyewitness to the French May, he searched for interpretative bearings amidst the smoke of an explosion spreading unstoppably from New York to Rome and from Mexico City to Tokyo. The revolt by the students who spontaneously faced off against police in the Latin Quarter, in the ancient alleyways around the Sorbonne, has a particular symbolic value. The overturned cars, the torn-down street signs and the torn-up cobblestones: the dream of revolution and the spectre of defeat resurfaced from the almost petrified depths of the riots of 1848 and the *journées* of the Paris Commune. References to the past multiplied, assuming an emblematic value. All the more so for Marcuse, who at barely twenty years of age had taken part in the Spartacist uprising in Berlin and participated in the armed defence of Alexanderplatz.

Thus, amidst the 'blaze' in Paris, Marcuse relived – perhaps a little bitterly – his own past experience. He particularly noted the graffiti on the walls, where the revolt articulated itself in the words of both Marx and Breton. The new slogan 'l'imagination au pouvoir' combined with the call for 'les comités (soviets) partout'.[21] For Marcuse, this reference was anything but indifferent. Even before this, he had been driven to think anew by the revolt of the black population in the United States, who daily suffered police violence (masked as 'control') on their own skin. Till the end, he would never tire of raising the alarm over the

49

concentration of the repressive apparatus, the double metamorphosis of police into military and military into police, which could only be held back by a diffuse revolt – a decentralized refusal.

Despite his implacable critique of capitalism, Marcuse remained bound to orthodox schemas and did not manage to decipher this revolt from below. The student movement was, perhaps, the 'ferment of hope', but it was not the working class, nor was it a vanguard able to break the vicious circle through which capitalism perpetuated itself by swallowing up all opposition.[22]

Spartacus's Day after Tomorrow

Furio Jesi's reading of revolt offers an exception to the usual way of understanding this term. In the pages of his *Spartakus*, published posthumously in 2000, the echoes of '68 (which he experienced first-hand) blend with those of the Spartacist uprising in Berlin, chosen as a starting point on account of its great emblematic value.

It all happened – everything played out – in the first fifteen days of 1919, at an accelerated pace that overwhelmed the lead actors themselves. In that terrible defeat, granted almost mythical status in the history of the left, it is possible to read the fragments of revolt in a reflected and condensed image.

Gunfire in the frozen Berlin night air. The Spartacists rose up, desperately fighting against the heinous lords of war, the ghastly money-owners, the wretched traitors to the working class, but also the monsters of the winter night and the demons of a city without solidarity, the overbearing granite symbol of the bosses. Remembering the German propaganda and the belligerent patriotism that had produced the barbarism of the world war, they rose up to escape the confines of the nation – to be Germans no longer. At every corner, at every crossroads, they opened fire on all those symbolic adversaries, those intangible enemies, without being able to confront them or flush them out. It was, therefore, a pure revolt, not dictated by the immediate political contingency but, rather, directed purely against the monstrous symbols of power. Fighting rather than defeating these demons was the important thing. Victory lay in the struggle itself.

The name Spartacus tellingly offered a present-day reference to the mythical past of slave revolt. The Spartakusbund, the Spartacist League, met for its congress on 31 December 1918 and that same day decided to found the German Communist Party. The leaders, including Rosa Luxemburg and Karl Liebknecht, looked favourably on the idea of running in the elections that were to be held shortly afterwards; they considered it necessary to break the national assembly from within, using it as a tribune from which to speak to the masses until they could attain a wider political maturity. Yet most delegates voted against the idea. 'Now or never!' The action seemed irrevocable. The revolt broke out even before the party could take its first steps – indeed, it ended up escaping the party's grip. This provided eloquent proof of the paradigmatic antithesis between party and revolt.

There were considerable revolutionary forces in Berlin. The aim was to conquer the symbols of power, occupying the newspaper buildings, the state printworks and the ministry of war. The rebels were convinced that this would spur the other German cities to action – and this did, in part, happen. But Friedrich Ebert's social-democratic government had already some time earlier concentrated ferocious troops and cavalry around Berlin. For days, thousands of worker combatants sacrificed their lives defending strategic positions – but these positions could not be held for long. On 9 January, under hails of machine-gun fire, the offices of the Spartacists' own organ *Die Rote Fahne* were abandoned. Luxemburg and Liebknecht had initially been averse to the uprising but remained side by side with the workers in revolt. They had no intention of running off somewhere else; instead, they took refuge in a neighbourhood where the counter-revolutionary troops did not dare to enter. Even amidst this predicament they wrote some articles, a survey of their dramatic experiences. False information led them to leave this safe refuge behind. On 15 January they were arrested and taken to the Hotel Eden. Liebknecht's corpse was dumped in an emergency room. As for Rosa Luxemburg, for a long time there would be no definite information. For months, the legend circulated in Berlin's working-class neighbourhoods that she had escaped and that she was still alive. This, until the spring, when her body re-emerged from the waters of the Landwehr canal, where she had been dumped.

Pummelled by the merciless blows of repression, the Spartacist revolt failed in the worst of all ways – out of its organizational incapacity and its gravely mistaken political perspective. The revolt did not seize hold of the symbols of power and nor did those behind it succeed even in limiting the scale of its defeat. The result in terms of the blood spilt was nothing short of disastrous. The Berlin proletariat lost its activists and the radical left almost all its leaders. In a very brief time-span, the tension that had built up over years – stirring a long and spasmodic expectation, perhaps even capable of bringing a revolution – was neutralized. Thus, it was possible to restore order, once and for all.

From this, it seems almost self-evident that we should draw a negative assessment of the revolt. But this is not the path that Jesi takes. He seeks not to judge the revolt from the standpoint of the success or failure of the revolution – not measuring it by the objectives it set itself – but, rather, to consider it on the basis of time. Indeed, this is revolt's own special province.

Improvised, unexpected and sudden, the revolt does not immediately fit into strategy unless, thanks to this later reframing, as the possible result of the design the revolution aims to make real. If a revolution always falls within historical time, revolt suspends this time and establishes a different one. In short: the revolt is the 'suspension of historical time'.[23] He avoids the term 'escape', which would be misleading – for it would suggest the idea of shrinking from the pain that history can inflict. That could also happen. But revolt is much more than that. Whoever takes part in a revolt will end up with a rare experience: for the refuge from historical time which she sought suddenly widens into a shared refuge. In the space and time and revolt, a whole community finds salvation.

Jesi admits to sticking by that widespread vision that distinguishes revolt from revolution, almost separating the two. Already in her day, Luxemburg had tended rather more to emphasize a continuity that made it possible to make out the germ of revolution within the revolt, to recover uprisings past, and to redeem defeats. In the days before her death, in an article that would become famous, she asked, 'Where would we be today without those "defeats"'![24]

Jesi operated within Marxism's dialectical schemas. He thus saw revolution as the outcome of an overcoming of the contradictions internal to capitalism and revolt as a serious strategic split, with negligible or even reactionary effects. Nonetheless, he did have one important insight. One could not stop at an external perspective, judging the revolt only by observing history and almost summoning it before the courts. The revolt ought to be considered on its own terms, in its autonomy, in its intensified experience of time. If the revolution prepares tomorrow, the revolt evokes the future that comes after tomorrow. It is thus a moment of striking consciousness, for it opens up a passageway into the future. This explains why it is of step with the present: whoever has no today can be driven to become the protagonist of the moment, to suspend historical time. This is an attempt which both forces things, like a sudden attack, and on the other hand neglects the question of the results, for it does not tend to its own survival. Constitutively out of step with the present, the revolt is an impatient epiphany of the future that comes after tomorrow.

The Limits of Public Space

Not all revolts have the same subversive charge. The difference does not lie only in their demands, their protagonists, the means they have at hand, or their chosen times and places. Rather, the decisive criterion is whether they situate themselves inside or outside – whether they respect the confines of public space or else blow up its frontiers. However unprecedented, creative and radical a revolt may be, it can still be said to be conventional so long as it remains within the prescribed limits. It is, conversely, subversive when it sows disorder in the political architecture, destabilizing and disrupting it. The conventional revolt plays out within established forms, at most introducing novel themes within the framework of public debate. The subversive revolt instead throws the very framework of politics into crisis.

It was Arendt who explicitly situated politics in the public space. In her reading, its birth is marked by the passage from the private sphere to the space in which individuals interact, where they show their faces and appear before one another. The *pólis* is not, as is generally believed, the city-state, meaning a space situated within a territory; rather, it is the 'space of appearance'.[25] In liberal democracies, this conception has enjoyed unchallenged success. This is also explained by the importance that the limelight takes on in the age of appearance. Doubtless, the nexus between politics and publicity has hardened to the point of becoming self-evident. This applies both to those who are inside – those with the faculty of appearing, or even of deciding who to let appear – and to those who are on the outside. Regardless of their other demands, many protests, demonstrations and occupations of public spaces insist on their right to appearance. For Butler, this takes place through an assembly of bodies which, as they come together in a bid for visibility, at the same time make this new 'body politic' recognizable.

Disaffected citizens fight for visibility and aim for recognition. Thus, rather than remain in the shadows or shut themselves away in silence, they seek means of access to the public space, so that they can formulate their claims and express their dissent in various ways. It goes without saying that this is also the space of democracy. The citizen who demonstrates – advancing her complaints and demanding her rights by way of words or gestures – exposes herself, publicly puts herself in contention, makes her entry into that space as a 'political subject', and thereby commits to share its rules, registers and codes. Even the disobedient are no exception. Despite the radicalism of the challenge, hers is a public act which, even in pushing up against the limits, makes up part of the democratic forms of protest.

The question does not change depending on whether we understand this space in deliberative or conflictual terms, as a site of discussion or an arena of confrontation. The long hegemonic model, whose most renowned defender is Jürgen Habermas, portrays a rational debate in which controversies are regulated and disputes and disagreements are negotiated. Communicative action is what makes democratic agreement possible.

Those who critique this – frankly irenic – model highlight the necessarily conflictual character of politics, invoking Schmitt and his famous statement that, for politics actually to exist, there needs to be an enemy. The enemy is not a competitor or an adversary; and, above all, he must be public and easily recognizable. Life and death are at stake here. Animosity is essential for identity: the ego becomes possible only through the immunitarian refusal of the other, identified as an enemy. It would, therefore, be a sign of inner turmoil, of duplicity, to have a variety of enemies or – and it is the same thing – not to be able to recognize one's own enemy. After all, this enemy provides the basis for the identity of the self, which would otherwise fragment and end up producing so many masks. *Aut–aut*, either–or – Schmitt thought in dichotomous terms. His politics of violence is an identity politics that calls for certain limits: hence his hydrophobia, his repugnance for the water, his aversion to the sea, the anarchic vastness that escapes the law of boundaries. The border is but the front line that defines the space of 'the political'.[26] This is the horizon of a final line of defences, a warlike clash – or, rather, something more akin to the duels of times past than contemporary warfare. The winds of sacrifice blow, a heroic pathos looms, a harsh tension dominates. It is difficult to imagine women finding a post on this front – and why should they?

So, according to the one perspective, intervention in the public space requires that one should be ready to converse and discuss face to face – or, according to the other perspective, it requires that one should be prepared for battle. But, in both cases, we remain stuck within pre-established frameworks. More than that, these frameworks are here confirmed and ratified. In general, it is presumed that a conflictual relationship à la Schmitt is the utmost expression of the radicalism that political conflict can reach; yet such a conflict involves no effective rupture between the sides. Conservative parties have often accused striking workers of jeopardizing the social bond; yet this bond is neither dissolved nor, still less, cut. Those who enter into conflict – with an individual, with a group, with an institution – are already situated within the public space, they accept its boundaries and conditions and articulate and mediate their antagonism according to those modalities.[27] They recognize the other – even if as an enemy – to whom they address themselves and from whom they demand a response. In so doing they confirm the existence of a reciprocal relationship. That is why, even when this struggle presents itself as rupture, it always ends up also marking a moment of integration.

Fundamental, here, is the idea that politics is circumscribed by the reciprocity of the public, physical or media stage. Whoever wants to enter that stage must be prepared to commit – that is, to sign their name, to risk their own hide, to put it all out there. They sign petitions, they intervene in assemblies, they participate in a demonstration. In this sense, they are putting themselves on display – and, indeed, fighting to do so.

The decisive commitment that the citizen has to make – is the pledge she has to offer, the price that she agrees to pay. It is no accident that we speak of political 'commitment'; it is taken for granted that politics has a cost. It is assumed that, if one is to enter within the bounds of public space and access the sphere of visibility, under the glare of the spotlights, one must accept the conditions, schemas and modalities of appearance. The committed citizen must accept the obligation tacitly demanded of her; when she appears in front of others, she has to be ready to answer for what she will do or say, to pay the possible price that her protest entails. Disagreement comes at a cost. This also applies in the most extreme conflict that can take place within the public space, within the boundaries of 'the political'. For here, too, the pledge has to be honoured; body, name and identity have to be committed, conditions have to be observed, and the bounds of this stage have to be respected.

Precisely because it draws on the theme of commitment, this conception of politics, which orients much of contemporary theory, seems to confer prestige on struggle and to attribute great importance to displays of disagreement. But, on closer inspection, commitment on the public stage is but a mechanism for neutralizing opposition, managing antagonism and governing the potential for conflict.

The Right to Appear

From the Arab Spring to the Indignados, from Occupy to Gezi Park, from Black Lives Matter to the women of Kobane, to NiUnaMenos – the movements beating their path through a globalized world are multiple, varied, but undeniably intense.

The word 'movement' could create misunderstandings. So it is worth specifying that this name does not suit well those groups which, having arisen off the back of the populist wave, take up a place not on the edges of politics but, instead, on the borders of the parties, in an ambiguous antithesis which is also a contiguity. This has mistakenly been spoken of as an 'anti-politics' – suggesting, among other things, that politics is limited to 'the parties, all of them corrupt, all part of the system, all exponents of "the caste"'. If that were so, the crisis of politics could be reduced to the corruption of individuals, a stain on representative democracy. Then it would suffice to replace the ruling political personnel, proposing citizen lists as an alternative to those presented by the traditional parties. With its inflamed language and its frequent recourse to rallies in town squares, so-called anti-politics presented itself as the long-awaited change. It led some to believe that – regardless of programmes, content, positions, indeed beyond left and right, as opportunity required – the decisive thing was the regulations, the methods, the rulebook. Thus anti-politics – trapped within the institutions, walled off within the electoral game – proved to be an extreme, paroxysmal attempt to conserve and restabilize the order of politics.

Movements see corruption very differently. They consider it symptomatic of a complex phenomenon rooted in the decline of representation and the hollowing out of political parties. These latter are now tasked with nothing more than the emergency management and administration of market diktats, under the threat of financial default.[28] The protest, therefore, has a rather different tenor. It interrogates the fate of democracy, pointing an accusing finger at the spaces of decision-making and the limits of politics. Thus, another vision emerges – one that is not only extra-institutional but takes up a place on the edges of politics. It questions the whole conceptual pattern with which modern political thought is woven, from the problem of sovereignty to the theme of the contract, from the idea of the nation to the notions of citizenship and state borders.

This is the light in which we should consider the movements that have made the city squares their key symbolic site. But what does it mean to meet, to be present, in the city squares? Judith Butler has raised this question.[29] Without overlooking the variety of public demonstrations, which are not always cause for confidence and hope (after all, the demonstrators may well be neo-fascists), Butler looks to what it is that 'holds together' these gatherings – meaning, to their salient political traits. In what she calls 'bodies in alliance', she makes out a form of resistance by a 'wounded life' that cannot bear unliveable conditions and can no longer tolerate mere survival. Coursing through the streets and squares, a mass comes together – one which political governance has not managed to govern, even when it dons its policeman's helmet. This is, therefore, the mass of the ungovernable, bursting onto the scene. Unrepresented by official politics, they thus lay claim to the public space, or, better, themselves reconfigure it, thanks to the performativity of bodies.

Just as politics blows up the old distinctions – for it now takes place also in neighbourhoods, in homes, in those spaces that were earlier relegated to the private sphere – the public space is not itself an abstract, static notion. A door is opened onto the 'between' of bodies, their acting in concert. Butler does not hesitate to speak of an 'interregnum', here indicating that new space that is constantly rearticulated in confrontation and the rupturing of the dominant relations. Though she is critical of Arendt – whose definition of politics is premised on the public–private split and thus perpetuates the old gendered boundaries – Butler does maintain the principle of appearance. To enter the public stage means to appear. This does not have to do only with its visual aspect: for voices, too, are important, and words are telling. Trying to break into the rigidly surveilled sphere of appearance are the today increasingly unseen and invisible expropriated, the poor relegated to a political as well as an economic destitution, the off-cast lives that power sees as so obscene. This is what happens when immigrant workers condemned as 'illegals' gather in the street, acting as if they were already citizens. In so doing they violate the boundaries of the public space and denounce its closure. For Butler, the contemporary squares politics revolves around the right to appearance – and it culminates in the famous chorus 'We, the people.'

Even apart from the theme of appearance, various questions are still left open – first off, the representative character of the 'we' that speaks of the people, for the people, without *being* the people. It cannot, therefore, impose itself and needs to be filled out.[30] But what also needs mentioning, here, is that this formula – which, not by accident, comes from the US constitution – always already expresses a constituent urge. Despite a certain 'interval', an 'act of splitting' to which Butler alludes, visible in 'We, the people', is the desire to affirm one's own sovereignty, assert one's own democratic legitimacy, arrogate oneself the right to self-government, faced with hollowed-out institutions, corrupt parties, and arbitrary and incompetent forces. The political community of 'us' – defined by nationhood and statehood – gathers in the square, as the myth of the contract is perpetuated.

A Volte-Face on Power

Already in his day, Spinoza recognized *indignatio* not as a simple passion, or just as an ethical reaction, but rather as a political response prompted by abuses of power (*Tractatus politicus*, IV, §6). When the sovereign violates the common interest, he sparks indignation among the citizenry.

It could be said that today's rage is an intensified form of an indignation that never went away. The geography of grievance has global dimensions – and a truly epochal endurance. Righteous anger is often isolated and flattened into personal demands, and it risks imploding in a swathe of micro-conflicts, dissipating amidst blind hatred. It can be daily absorbed by the market, with the result that there is no residue of subversion that might compromise the ultimate horizon of capitalism – this semi-solar system constantly able to present itself in ever renewed eternal metamorphosis.

Revolt requires a politics of indignation. This implies both collective action and recollection – a passage not only in space but also in time. Individual grievances are gathered together and a shared tension is built, raising the common gaze to history to try, if not to tear it from its binding, then at least to leave the required, desired future written on one of its pages.

When indignation takes to the squares, it is looking for power. The efforts to stigmatize it, which reduce it to an episode in nihilism devoid of any political meaning and wedded to destruction, overlook this quest, this intention. Often emphasized by media, the attack on the symbols of planetary governance – from bank branches to the windows of luxury retailers – ought to be read in this light. This is not so much an intensification of burning passions as an open challenge to power or, even better, a bid to meet face to face. As she covers her face, the demonstrator seeks to unmask the hidden face of power. The square becomes the site of this encounter, ever on the brink of exploding into an open clash. Politics appears distant, abstract, disembodied, devitalized; for which reason bodies put themselves into contention, as they try to force power to become bodily and visible, to show itself in its most violent institutional form – that is, the forces of order. Finally, power is there, just a step away, behind the visor of the riot helmet protecting the policeman. This clash provides the impression of finally being in contact with power, embodied in the brutality of the sovereign police, which gives politics a body and a face. Through the streets, in the squares, this policing politics brushes up against citizens' bodies, when it is not injuring or arresting them. Power has taken off its mask.

Yet this possibility of provoking power, touching it, striking it, almost grabbing hold of it, neglects its more sneaky, sophisticated, ruthless forms. From the clash in the square echoes the question: 'Where is power?' It could be said that this confrontation is the attempt to localize power, to identify its place – that is, to unveil its secret. Moreover, the revolutionary gesture *par excellence* is to locate the site of power precisely in order to keep it at a distance, to shake off its control, and at the same time to prepare an attack against it.

The critical question 'Where is power?' – the problem from which the present crisis of politics largely springs – remains unanswered in the democracies of the age of globalization. This is not because power has gone away; if anything, it is exercised even more energetically than ever before. Rather, it remains unanswered because the source of power can no longer be situated in any particular place. As we know, democracy is the offspring of the abandonment of the royal schema of the body politic in which everything was concentrated in the sovereign. In the democratic system, political power is constantly subjected anew to the test of electoral suffrage.

Yet, in present-day democracy, power – distant and divided from its popular source – appears ever more indistinct. Fleeting, ubiquitous, networked, projected across the webs of technology and the flows of the economy, lacking any centre and perhaps any direction, it has no face, no name, no address. Yet, for all that, this soft power is no less violent. The malaise felt by those struck by this power lies precisely in their difficulty in locating it. They perceive only its diffuse presence. From this derives the crisis of representation. The citizen feels tricked by the way in which power shows itself on official occasions; she thus becomes uncertain, wary, suspicious. If there is such and such effect – it is to be supposed metaphysically – then this must also have a cause. Scepticism turns into the dogmatic certainty that there is some hidden lair of power. Thus emerge the dark conspiracy fantasies that infest the political landscape. These only multiply when 'the king has no clothes', and even when – as in the Greek crisis – the power that governs the realm of the planetary economy cannot but show its face.

In their two symmetrical visions, Claude Lefort and Michel Foucault suggested that power should be understood in relational terms. Lefort maintained that, in contemporary democracy, power is an 'empty site' – an atopic one, which is thus not unreal but, rather, absent. Foucault constantly sought out power in the clinic, in the prison, in disciplining institutions, in all those spaces on the margins, which he called heterotopias, where power is experienced differently, where it exercises itself even on bodies through its 'microphysics'. Both men shared the conviction that it is impossible to localize power, which on closer inspection is both everywhere and nowhere, on each occasion inhabiting a different site in which it functions in a different way.

It could be said that metaphysics still prevails – and that this has prevented the full abandonment of the myth of power. If power is not a property of the powerful or a possession of those who govern, then the expropriation of the governed appears in a different light. This is all the more true when we also consider – as we should – the temporal aspect of power, seeing that it is not only a relation but an event. A striking aspect of today's revolts is that, apart from the actual staging of the confrontation, the question of place passes onto a secondary plane; the revolt is an event that drives people to take to the squares, thus dislodging power from its supposed centrality, and recognizing its emptiness, its fundamental absence. This dislocation is decisive.

The formula 'destituent power' was first introduced in 2001 by the Colectivo Situaciones of Buenos Aires. It used this term to characterize the *píqueteros* movement, whose name comes from the pickets used to interrupt the city's economic-political flows.[31] It thus refers to an aspect that transcends the traditional forms of protest, civil disobedience included. The protest to which it refers is not an anxious bid to grasp hold of power but, rather, a move to escape its grip.

A wide-ranging debate has opened up around the idea of 'destitution'.[32] The Invisible Committee especially breathed life into this theme in philosophical and, above all, political terms.[33] The prefix 'de' indicates a distancing motion, a deposing action; yet it still retains a certain juridical-bureaucratic note in the verb *statuere*, which belongs to the state lexicon of statehood and institutional activity. But we would do better to recover the meaning of the Italian word *rivolta* – that is, not a face-to-face confrontation but, rather, a turning away, marking a change of side and a break from command. Looking at the kaleidoscope of new revolts, with all the destituent spirit they display, we can try to follow these escape routes.

Prefigurations

The wind of protest blows through cities, one after another. This ought not surprise us. The history of revolutionary movements has always unfolded in the urban context, where capital is concentrated and political power condensed. Benjamin touched on this theme already in his *Arcades Project*. Squares, streets and alleyways are the fitting – almost ritual – setting for marches, demonstrations and barricades. This has not changed even in today's context, in which global metropoles, which many now consider a vanguard running ahead of the state, seem to contain an innovative potential in the webs that bring them together.[34]

But conflict does not slip only from the factory to the city square. The transition is a both wider and deeper process: the new revolts revolve around the question of inhabiting. This turn does not imply that the fight over the ownership of the means of production has gone away; but the problem of work can no longer be addressed without also considering the questions of technology and territory. Inhabiting ought to be understood not as the possession of a habitation but, rather, as a political-existential relationship to the self, to others, to the earth. How ought one reside and cohabit?

In this regard, it is worth dwelling for a moment on the ZADs – an acronym for the French term *Zones à défendre* ('areas to defend'). On the one hand, this label subverts the administrative term *Zone d'aménagement différé* ('designated development area'), referring to areas where the state has a right of first refusal or sale. On the other, it hints tellingly at the acronym ZAT (in English, TAZ, Temporary Autonomous Zone), a concept successfully advanced by the anarchist writer Hakim Bey in the early 1990s.[35] The ZADs are, in general, areas illegally occupied out of opposition to agro-industrial programmes or controversial projects, such as the building of an airport or a car park, or construction works for a high-speed railway line or fracking site. But they are not only defensive in character: they are also spaces where the *zadistes* try to develop alternative forms of inhabiting space, respectful of natural resources and solidarity. Beyond the European context, there have also been experiments with autonomous zones in various Latin-American regions, where *indios* have often been leading actors in struggles against multinationals. We can also speak of even more extensive such zones in Chiapas and Kurdistan.

In political terms, the ZADs are important both because they represent resistance to projects imposed by an often short-sighted and opportunistic territorial planning practices and because they are the prefiguration of radically democratic and ecological forms of inhabiting the world. Prefiguration does not only mean showing that the current world is not the best possible one. Autonomous zones, for years already discussed in anarchist thought, are a bid to open up an 'outside' – they are, so to speak, a trial run at decapitalization.[36]

This may sound incautiously naive. But such an assessment would neglect the dual value of the autonomous zones which, in their quest for the broken link between politics and existence, hint at another way of understanding the kinetics of revolution. It is pointless to think of revolution, imagined as the storming of the Winter Palace, in the expectation that *this* will change our lives; for forms of life can change already. In this sense, these zones attest to the need to break out of this vicious circle.

An Existential Tension

Revolt is usually analysed in terms of its political charge, while the existential tension that both permeates and underpins it is left overlooked. No one has yet outlined – if not by way of occasional hints – a phenomenology of revolt that unpacks its individual perspective.

The only way to understand this tension is to start out from the fragile connection between politics and existence, which withered already some time ago. In this light, revolt is first of all a response to the abstraction of politics, which is now reduced to a consensus calculation, a bureaucratic procedure, a pragmatic adaptation to the world's onward march. Revolt seeks somehow to recover this connection, often by dramatizing its loss.

Through the streets and squares, the existential malaise explodes, bringing out the apprehension, anxiety and unease that institutional politics pretends to ignore. Thus a demonstration does not stop at asserting a demand: it is always also an exasperated way of showing power the effects that it has on the body and the mind. In this sense, the uprising motion also means standing up from depressed torpor; it is a way of reclaiming dignity.

Those who take to the squares have the intoxicating sensation that they have suddenly become protagonists of their own existence – that they are finally in the

73

presence of history, standing at the crossroads where its course will be decided. Here is the breach, the long-awaited opening towards an outside which, amidst the suffocating smog of capitalism, had seemed closed forever. Revolt is already experienced as the beyond – at least, that is, so long as the tension holds up. Revolt is, therefore, an intensified present in which the passageway to the future opens.

The revolt is a dizzying burst of intensity in an existence which is otherwise closed in on itself, relegated to the passivity of a spectator, caught in impotence and doomed to inauthenticity. The revolt is a nervous awakening, a stirring of emotion, an exposure to the limits, an extension that breaks with monotony and interrupts grey continuity. Revolt is, therefore, a sensation of existing. The intensity of the revolt is the fortress of existential resistance.

The temporary goodbye to everyday hardship, the step away from it, is a sort of exile or, better, a disidentification. The widespread use of masks, scarves and hoods should not be ascribed to security concerns alone. By putting on these garments, the self casts off and forgets itself, hides the person behind the mask and conceals them in all colours of blackness as it awaits a new beginning. The 'subject' of the revolt does not put themselves on display or seek to display themselves as such; instead, they unite with others as they assimilate into a solidaristic alliance of bodies. It is as if they all make up one opaque body, which can nonetheless clearly express itself. Those who have nothing to lose and no side to defend, those who are denied the right of appearance, paradoxically put their own invisibility on show. At the same time, they use invisibility as an escape route, spectacularizing and parading it. They carry this wrong into the public space.

In the aesthetic of revolt – an attempt to force open the barriers enclosing the space of politics – this dissimulation of the self is sometimes accompanied by a simulation of the world's chaos, in which burning Molotovs and colourful flares are means of breaking out of illegibility. What emerges in either case is the demand to see things clearly – the revolt's aspiration for lucidity.

If Dissent is a Crime

Why does almost every form of conflict seem to slip outside of the framework of legality? The turn from shop-floor protests to the city squares has also entailed a transformation, and a widening, of the issues at stake, from the economic question of wages to the biopolitical question of inhabiting space.

Demands over working conditions remain as important as ever. But if the legal framework for struggle is itself a proud achievement of the workers' movement, these forms have gradually lost their intensity and are all but doomed to decline. This applies to the whole multifaceted array of tools in the trade-union repertoire – and in particular the strike. While strikes continue to be effective, now that they have become something close to an institutional praxis they no longer have the disruptive force that they once did. Trade unions nonetheless remain key to struggles over wages; their role is especially fundamental when we consider the structural, decades-long crisis of parties now wholly unable to mobilize citizens.

While demonstrations had long been illegal, the right to demonstrate is now recognized as a fundamental democratic freedom. Yet it has lost its spontaneous character and has largely lost its subversive charge, as it has been tamed and absorbed into the juridical, organizational and political framework. The police authorities authorize and surveil demonstrations, while the traditional organizations (trade unions, parties, partisan associations, etc.), and often also the movements, call and coordinate them (not always with the desired results). It may even be the case – as in France on 11 January 2015, following the *Charlie Hebdo* attack – that a large demonstration for freedom of expression, led by a parade of heads of government, can serve as a pretext for declaring a state of emergency that itself destroys freedoms.

But, while demonstrations have been tamed, this does not tell us that conflict has disappeared or that society has been pacified. Rather, just as the contents of struggle constantly change, so, too, do its forms. That which governance does not succeed in institutional-izing is simply expelled from the terrain of legality, and criminalized. There is thus a constant redrawing of the boundary between what is admitted in the public space and what is banished from it. Alongside legal protests, there is a proliferation of extra-legal struggles which, though relegated to the margins, are assuming increasing significance.[37] Even the tendency to criminalize these struggles is unable to stop the centre of gravity of conflict inexorably exceeding and destabilizing public space.

The protagonists of extra-legal struggles have many different faces. They range from online activists raising the alarm from cyberspace, to ZAD militants seeking to develop new ways of inhabiting space, to the new 'disobedients' with their sometimes audacious actions. And then there are those active in NGOs operating in cross-border spaces – the stretches of open sea, where they still raise the banner of justice and the flag of humanity. When they come to the aid of migrants and offer help to the refugees in the camps, they also face a barrage of fire trying to neutralize them.

This tells us that it is not only militants, driven to invent new forms of struggle, who are being expelled from the space of legality but also people doing human-itarian work – a kind of activity which ought instead to be recognized and appreciated.

Recent political and judicial developments thus shine a light on the state's leading role in criminalizing and thus depoliticizing conflict. As the state mounts its sovereign, securitarian turn, it is ready both to declare the illegality of acts once considered as democratic rights or duties and to criminalize those who do venture to take such actions. With this bitter, resentful sovereignty, the state prepares the ground for repression. But it ends up getting caught in unprecedented dilemmas which necessarily implicate democracy itself.

Are the new 'disobedients' terrifying outlaws who ought to be tried and punished? Or are they model citizens whose bold initiatives are to be thanked for reinvigorating democracy? Are they a threat to public order, or are they allowing the law to rediscover its lost sense of justice? These are each ways of summing up a question that has gradually made its way onto the agenda.[38]

Disobedience is valuable not only under despotic regimes. It is the core of democracy itself. Citizens are not subjects; and, for this reason, they cannot tamely accept a law that disavows not only constitutional limits but the limits of humanity itself. It is as if it were obvious that life-saving should be criminalized and as if turning ethics on its head is only to be expected: those who work to save human lives are held guilty of hurting them. Where the defence of human rights is considered an act of subversion, democracy is at risk of collapse. The accusation of subversive behaviour is a mere pretext. Those who disobey are not violating the law, but challenging it. And they challenge it in the name of a higher Law – a betrayed Constitution and a justice that has gone missing.

The New Disobedients

Yawning inequalities, the rampant spread of the principle of indebtedness, irreversible environmental destruction, the unknowns of technological acceleration … if we look at the conditions in the world today, it ought to be surprising that there is such obedience.

The new forms of protest can be considered acts of civil disobedience. But in some cases – the most unprecedented – they go beyond this and exceed disobedience even in its most radical sense. Through its innately conflictual character, disobedience is the opposite of resignation, inertia, passivity, and delegation to others. Citizens can no longer leave it up to others to take the initiative and shy away from tasks which they must themselves fulfil. So, it is necessary to rise up. The new disobedients know that they are disobeying – and often they openly embrace this fact.

Ever since the mid-twentieth century, disobedience – so unjustifiably absent during the Nazi era – has returned to the headlines and fuelled a philosophical, political and juridical debate that remains yet to be exhausted. Indeed, in recent years it has become ever more intense. In this context, too, the turn was also coloured by the totalitarian experience. The zealous obedience of the agent impeccably executing his orders was exposed in all its monstrosity. All the more so, given that the rationale that these agents obeyed was not that of universal rights but, rather, the cold, anonymous rationality of impersonal calculation.

Faced with the 'monsters of obedience' – the likes of Adolf Eichmann, who planned the logistics of the 'Final Solution' and in 1961 declared in court that he had simply been following orders – the question took on different contours. To obey does not mean having no accountability to anyone and nothing to answer for. Those who tamely submitted seemed to have abandoned all responsibility. Eichmann's 'thoughtlessness' – in Arendt's famous formula – lay precisely in his lack of judgement, in his reliance on commonplaces, in the automatism of his speech. This is where his real guilt lies: in his preference not to know, not to see, not to think. If what happened then had again repeated itself, how many children of Eichmann would have jeopardized democracy itself? The technical-bureaucratic organization of life, which divided up the responsibility, making them indifferent and anaesthetized, would have facilitated the efforts of future grey executioners, without either souls or mercy.[39]

In postwar years, Immanuel Kant was himself called into the dock, given the rigid formalism of his ethics. Yet, even when he praised obedience, he had not failed repeatedly to invoke the need for vigilance. Moreover, the courage of critical judgement – up to and including civil dissent – pervades and agitates the entire Western tradition. Philosophy keeps the attention on alert. How could anyone forget the case of Socrates? Unjustly accused and unjustly condemned, he refused to flee, as he instead submitted to the laws of the *pólis*. Yet, while he accepted the sentence, he did not grant it legitimacy. His singular obedience was a form of resistance, which lay the ground for all the future dissent that was to come. In Socrates, the disobedient 'no' – which is also a 'yes' to one's own conscience – found its voice.

But this picture would be left entirely incomplete if it did not also take into account the American face of disobedience, as personified by Henry David Thoreau and the extraordinary biography of the African-American civil rights movements. These movements reached their peak in the epoch-defining march on Washington in 1963, at which Martin Luther King Jr. gave his most famous speech, 'I have a dream'. Those years saw not only conventional marches but also the spread of a new practice deployed by protestors: the sit-in. This practice had first been introduced in shop-floor struggles, with the victorious strike against General Motors in 1937 – an action known as the sit-down strike. This meant not striking and leaving the premises but, rather, striking and remaining in place. Similarly, African-American protestors – with their movement's long history of turning to flight and migration in order to escape from slavery – now used the sit-in as a means of ostentatiously defying segregationism. This could mean entering 'off-limits' premises, sitting down on the pavement, not reacting to violence, and letting themselves be dragged off by the police, or even to jail. This sequence of protest thus reckoned with the possibility of arrest. In not a few cases, the jails did not have enough space for the huge numbers of demonstrators. This form of 'non-violent civil disobedience' proved particularly effective. As well as dramatizing and exposing the otherwise hidden tension in US society, it tried to shake white people's sluggish conscience, so that they would break out of the dark depths of racism and convert to the cause of justice.

In a different part of the world, already some years previously Mohandas K. Gandhi had drawn inspiration from Thoreau's pages as he made 'non-violent resistance' the calling card of a new politics. The context was different, and so, too, was the goal: to take power from the British imperialists and give it to the Indian people. Disobedience became the non-violent violation of the state's iniquitous, oppressive, immoral laws. This was a permanent challenge to the political order which did not resort to force, or still less arms; rather, it submitted to incarceration and other types of violence perpetrated by the authorities. It thus fostered democracy and could harm only an autocratic state that feared public opinion. Gandhi went so far as to say that disobedience was an 'inalienable right of the citizen'. And he maintained that it should be considered the purest form of agitation within the limits of the constitution.[40]

This latter point is itself decisive. It is no accident that the version of civil disobedience provided by John Rawls – destined to become the dominant synthesis also in liberal circles – emphasizes its limits. The concern, here, is to soften any cause for disturbance, erase the gesture of defiance, and banish any 'danger of anarchy'.[41] While disobedience was still for Martin Luther King Jr. 'civil', because it exposed the incivility of an American society based on racist segregation, here it becomes civilized, tamed, 'conscientious'. Rawls sees disobedience as a non-violent expression of public-mindedness, clashing with the law but carried out 'within the limits of fidelity to law'.[42] Those who disobey appeal to the sense of justice of the government and the majority, in order to change and improve things in the name of the shared political principles that regulate the Constitution. Ultimately, far from being a revolutionary, the disobedient is an honest reformer.

Two prerogatives thus emerge: publicity and responsibility. This is not so much a matter of the distinction between group and individual, as emphasized by

Arendt.[43] The important thing is that the action – even if it is an individual one – should take place in the public space, out in the open. Publicity is the hinge on which disobedience turns: it has to make the iniquity of a law plain for all to see. It aims to change or get rid of this law, addressing fellow citizens, their opinion and, at the most fundamental level, their consciences. In this sense, disobedience is both an ethical and a political appeal to civil society, calling on it to live up to its own principles.

It is, therefore, a responsible act – and, indeed, one that takes an extra degree of responsibility. Those who blatantly transgress some decree in the name of justice answer for this by putting the authenticity of their commitment to the test – and preparing to pay the price. State repression is not long in coming. The disobedient does not run away but, rather, recognizes the legitimacy of this state intervention. This itself demonstrates the violence of the authority that punishes her. It is as if reaching the jail cell is the final goal, setting the seal on her struggle.

Indeed, the famous night that Thoreau spent in jail is an emblematic scene in the history of disobedience. It happened on 23 July 1846. The eccentric walking philosopher, who led a secluded life in a cabin on the edge of Walden Pond, headed to Concord that morning to collect a pair of boots he was getting repaired; a sheriff stopped him, reminding him of the debt he had for years owed to the state of Massachusetts. Thoreau reacted indignantly: even apart from the scandalous policy on slavery in the Southern states, the tax that he was meant to pay was meant to finance a fresh unjust war with Mexico. He thus refused to pay: 'Under a government which imprisons any unjustly, the true place for a just man is also a prison.'[44]

Disobedience comes at a price, not only because it challenges the hierarchies of power, thus underlining the discord between law and justice, but also because it interrupts the monotony of submission. Why do the submissive obey? This is the question Étienne de la Boétie raises in his pamphlet on voluntary servitude.[45] The answer lies in the chain of complicity: they accept being tyrannized so that they can themselves tyrannize and accept subjugation so that they can themselves subjugate others. Thus, the obedient get even by settling for a small part in the mechanism of power. Yet this is a mechanism that also undermines democracy itself.

Legitimate, difficult and risky, civil disobedience is a political challenge and an ethical obligation. It requires the courage not to betray oneself and the justice one believes in by folding to the iniquitous command of others. This means that, within disobedience, there is always also a form of obedience, to one's own conscience. The act of those who say 'no' cannot, therefore, be interpreted as a criminal act. Disobedience is, rather, an obligation in a world where responsibility has fragmented, indifference exonerates anyone from having to react, and the prevalent political impotence is taken for a sovereign neutrality. That is why some speak of an 'unlimited responsibility'.[46]

Yet, even this sharp tension does not exceed the limits of public space, the binds of the law, the confines of the Constitution. Even the most rebellious of disobedients play the game and do not abandon this field. Arendt emphasizes this repeatedly; this reflects her concern to demonstrate the constitutionality and democratic spirit of disobedience as compared to other, violent forms of protest, as well as her embarrassment over a latent subversive charge that she can hardly ignore. Arendt thus ends up identifying disobedience as a symptom indicative of the instability of democratic systems and the erosion of governmental authority; it is almost the antechamber of a revolutionary situation.[47] But for Arendt, as for Marcuse (albeit from a different perspective), there is a discontinuity between the two. It is impossible to make out the passage from antechamber into the chamber itself, although the antechamber is nonetheless attributed an ancillary role.

Yet, the problem lies precisely in the constitutionality that Arendt so praises. Civil disobedience is that revolt which remains within the limits of the public space conceded by liberal democracy. In this sense, it is the most intensified, most radically democratic – or democratically radical – practice, which makes the most seditious possible use of the law, the Constitution and the state, as it launches its challenge from within their bounds. Derrida captured this insightfully in his essay on Mandela.[48]

But disobedience does not go further. It does not put into question the political architecture of liberal democracy; it does not interrogate the governance of the public space or break with the *Rechtsstaat*. The sit-in represents all this in the most clarifying of ways – indeed, it is the means of action held up as the symbol of disobedience. In this light, it is difficult to consider even Thoreau as a disobedient. This owes not so much to a famous ambiguity (his work was originally entitled 'Civil Resistance to Government') as to the fact that he forcefully (if abstractly) asserted the need to dissociate himself from the state – that is, the possibility of breaking out of the state framework.[49]

Hence the novelty of the 'new disobedients', who operate on the limits of public space, on the margins of the community, and every now and then cross these limits – whether by land or by sea – thereby shaking the political architecture and destabilizing the state-centric order. It is no accident that they rescue, aid and welcome migrants, and nor is it any accident that they are criminalized and accused of illegality. Their disobedience already crosses the border into anarchist revolt.

Anonymous's Grin

It would be impossible to retrace its first steps; they are lost in the dark, meandering paths of the web, in the ghettoes of 4chan's /b/ electronic noticeboard, where users could comment and participate in the discussion without identifying themselves. They were assigned the nickname 'anonymous', but they increasingly identified with Anonymous. Popular cyberculture – inspired by the figure of the troll and her provocative, deceptive interventions – gradually blended with libertarian currents among hackers. Already in their encounter with alterglobalization, these latter had made their political commitment and become hacktivists. All this produced an unusual mix. But it was also a moment of redemption – for from the roughest peripheries of the web emerged Anonymous, one of the most subversive movements on the contemporary landscape. Anonymous is a non-collective collective, an unbranded brand, and a name that does not refer to anyone, available to all.

'No one speaks for Anonymous. Nothing is official. No videos. No operations. Not even this press release, even though it was created by an Anonymous number of Anonymous at an Anonymous time in an Anonymous place and uploaded Anonymously, it does not speak for Anonymous.' So we read on one of its most important information channels, the website anonnews.org.

This gives us a sense of why it is so hard to reconstruct its history. It first hit the headlines around the world in January 2008 when it launched an attack against Scientology, which it accused of having had troubling footage of Tom Cruise taken down from the internet. Here, the focus was on censorship and religious manipulation. This attack was followed by a message that went viral. 'Hello, leaders of Scientology. We are Anonymous. ... You have nowhere to hide because we are everywhere. ... Knowledge is free. We are Anonymous. We are Legion. We do not forgive. We do not forget. Expect us.' Perhaps those speaking here were 'cyberterrorists', as Fox News had branded them in a chilling 2007 report. Or were they the latest exponents of the centuries-old tradition of freethinking? Batted between contradictory judgements, public opinion showed a certain indulgence when, in a move to strengthen its initiative against the Scientologists, on 10 February 2008 Anonymous decided to take to the streets for the first time, in over a hundred cities around the world. From London to Los Angeles the demonstrators appeared in the mask of V, the legendary protagonist of *V for Vendetta*. The mask was simultaneously both a shield to ward off reprisals and a shared code which allowed individuals arriving from cyberspace to come together. This could be termed a masterstroke in terms of capturing media attention. From then on, V became the Anonymous mask.

There have been various misadventures, owing both to anonymity and to Anonymous's open horizontalism. Feeding both uncertainties and outright splits, this has sometimes led Anons – as the activists are called – to turn on their own side. But Anons have nonetheless continued their far-reaching efforts in defence of rights and freedom of information. Decisive in this story was their alliance with the programming genius Julian Assange, who himself hails from the hacker community. Thanks to its global political vision, WikiLeaks – which stands for anonymity and the opening up of public information to citizens – was able to provided Anonymous with its theoretical bearings. Their image thus shifted, from fanatical pirates to new Robin Hoods of the web. In December 2010 came 'Operation Avenge Assange', launched by AnonOps, one of the most militant networks. Through massive simultaneous access requests, it succeeded in jamming the websites of big financial firms such as PayPal and Mastercard after they suspended donations to WikiLeaks.

No less significant was the move into the city squares. On 15 May 2011, when the indignados invaded Madrid's Puerta del Sol, Anonymous did not hesitate in taking a stand. A few months later, on 15 October 2011, they sided with Occupy Wall Street, offering it media visibility via their own digital channels. This was also an opportunity to make the hackers' world known and bring it closer to the protest. Anons thus appeared side by side with trade unionists. The V masks that studded the squares and the web sealed an unprecedented convergence, almost a cross-contamination, between spontaneous assemblies which tried to occupy the stage and subversive movements arriving from cyberspace.

Since then, Anonymous has assumed an ever more important role in the media sphere and has inspired similar initiatives, as in the case of cyberfeminism. There have been countless operations: in the Arab Spring, and against repressive regimes in general – from Iran to Turkey and Syria – not to mention the attacks against the Ku Klux Klan, white supremacists, and far-right groups and parties. There was an impressive action against the jihadist universe around ISIS. Anons have claimed responsibility for all manner of attacks on websites and forums spreading child pornography. They have been a constantly vigilant watchdog of financial institutions, banks, pharma companies, the food industry and, indeed, abuses by the forces of order.

It could be said that the tactic pursued by Anonymous centres on interruption – an interruption which happens on multiple levels, though they often converge. Key, in this regard, are the lols (literally, laugh out loud), through humour or pranks. The best means of subversion is not to destroy but, rather, to alter the code. A similar practice is DDoS (standing for

Distributed Denial of Service) attacks, which temporarily jam a site. Here, classic modes of protest, from the street blockade to the sit-in, are transposed into the virtual space. Halfway between pranks and doxing (spreading information and data) is the now rather frequent practice of defacement: a site is defaced either to show how insecure the information hosted there is, or for some symbolic purpose. This happened in the week around 5 November 2019, when the homepages of various European far-right sites were replaced with the V mask.

Anonymous is a movement without hierarchies, managers or leaders. It is impossible to make your name in its ranks, grow famous, become a public figure, or promote yourself according to the canons of individualism that dominate the political scene. We find confirmation of this in the iconography it has adopted – not just the mask but also the image of a person in a suit and tie with a question mark where their head should be. Anyone can be Anonymous, taking on the name of anonymity. But its radical openness, its free availability to all, ought not be misunderstood. Though Anonymous may have no organization, it does exhibit both cultural cohesion and political solidarity.[50] It functions like a meme, a reusable character. The capital A invokes the possibility of an infinite number. Anarchist decentralization flourishes also in its means of action. There are neither leaders nor

orders. An impermanent community unites spontaneously around some temporary aim, like a shoal of fish
that move together in the depths of the ocean or a flock
of birds emigrating in the same direction. Nothing
stops them separating or joining back together again.
The movement's anonymous horizontality is both its
strength and its weakness. If even the so-called Anons
are arrested, Anonymous would continue to be shared.

Fascination alternates with apprehension. It is unsur-
prising that, in the hypercodified space of politics, this
movement – like other similar ones – is either under-
estimated or else ostracized and criminalized. Especially
under accusation is its practice of anonymity: held to
be illegal, it is in turn depoliticized. Yet fundamentally
there is also a moral judgement at work here.

Obviously, the use of anonymity as a shield also means
evading any potential sanctions. In this perspective,
a 'politics of anonymity' would be a contradiction in
terms. If one does not accept the need to appear in
public, as an identifiable actor, then one ends up placing
oneself outside the political stage. But this is precisely
the dilemma that Anonymous wants to explode. This,
in turn, means shaking off the conventional political
framework – hence why, given the destabilizing effects
of their activity, they are the target of often dispropor-
tionate repression.

Yet, anonymity seems not only desirable but almost
a necessity. We could find many examples of this. It is

hard to understand why those who denounce abuse, embezzlement and fraud should have to pay a price for this, exposing themselves to sacking, demotion, reprisals or other even worse consequences,[51] especially when they are not directly involved in the anomalies or malpractice they highlight. But, in this, the idea again emerges that those who commit to some cause must also be prepared to provide some collateral in return. The role of those who conform is thus counterposed to the anomalous role of those who dissent. Ultimately, dissent is passed off as a choice, and a choice you have to pay for. Those who make that choice have, on this reading, always already committed themselves to the restrictions imposed by the public space and submitted to the obligations of the political architecture – obligations supposedly guaranteeing that the cost will be reimbursed, the associated penalties made good.

As well as questioning such a vision of dissent, it is worth asking why anyone should have to resort to such an expedient as anonymity in a democracy – which, as such, ought not to impose any pre-emptive censorship or throw up obstacles to the possibility of acting and expressing oneself. The result is to reduce drastically the numbers who do participate; indeed, not everyone is so inclined to take the risk and to pay the price. The nexus between politics and publicity intensifies the choreography of the public stage, heightening its tension. The practice of anonymity, conversely, takes the drama out of matters and, denouncing these restrictions, hints at a politics beyond the schemas that organize the public space.

The Anons have already put this possibility on display. With their breakthrough onto the public stage, they subvert the modes of protest. No one knows who suddenly started doing this, or where – still less who will keep it going, where or how. Anyone can take part from one moment to the next, even just a little, without having to align themselves. The protest is nomadic, temporary, fragmentary. Together with the multiplication of times there is also an increasing diversity of places – for protest no longer sticks to the spaces previously assigned to mobilization. This also corresponds to the decentralization that comes with the web. The space of protest is no longer institutionalized, monopolized by the forces of order, managed by the traditional intermediaries (parties, unions) or granted to certain accepted groups and movements. Anonymous's success lies in its diffuse spread of spaces and in its redistribution of democracy itself.

Anonymous has had an even more explosive effect on the 'subject', who is, of course, unidentifiable. On the public stage, individuals are generally driven to present themselves not only with a properly documented identity but also an easily recognizable one. Where the play of interactions intensifies and conflict sharpens, identity is crystallized and fixed. This is plain to see in the case of so-called public figures but also with the ordinary activist or sympathizer. The practice of anonymity is a de-subjection – in many senses. First of all because it frees individuals from subjection to the surrounding institutional framework, but also because it lifts them up from that resigned submission in which they end up swallowing a rigid self-image which has been reflected back to them by others. As well as a protection from external pressures, anonymity, like the mask, offers freedom from identity. Or, better, in unmasking the myth of identity, it allows the shattering of that identity which always already impairs existence. This means dis-identifying, un-belonging – and cultivating robust forms of resistance.

The name Anonymous breaks open the politics of identity, smashes through the limits of the landscape outlined by Schmitt, and transgresses the warlike logic rooted in the politics of identity. In that context, the self cannot have any other faces and, being easily recognizable, must be ready to fight. But the practice of anonymity invokes the possibility of acting politically without entering into the classic framework of conflict. And this makes it far more conflictual.

Anonymity means intervening without either being recognized or recognizing the enemy. The atypical formula 'Greetings, citizens of the world, we are Anonymous' is indeterminate as to either its author or its addressee; it does not aspire to a shared 'we' or aim at the constitution of a 'people'. This points to a decisive difference from those protest movements that culminate in the chorus 'We, the people', affirming its own sovereignty. Anonymous's greetings head in a different direction. This is not only because they are addressed to all, but also because they are the meeting point of erratic alliances. These do not harden into a 'we' but, rather, try to break individuals out of the schemas of belonging, the identitarian passion, and the sovereign mania. And, in so doing, they give rise to an archipelago of open, heterogeneous communities in revolt.

On Invisibility: A Show of Self-Concealment

Anonymity is the response to the politics of identification. It is thus closely connected with the use of masks. This is a matter not simply of self-concealment but of using self-concealment to show oneself. This is a challenge to the state which condemns all masks other than its own, a challenge to faceless financial power and a disembodied economy which disregards its own effects. The enormous asymmetry is put on display, the disparity of forces brought out into the open. But, above all, this is a refusal of the planetary surveillance, a claim to the right to opacity.

Across history there is no lack of examples analogous to Anonymous, where movements sought a fictional name that could provide a cover for their actions. Indeed, this is a truly ancient tradition, dating back to the first revolts of the poor. Take the example of the *jacquerie*, the popular uprising in France named with reference to the epithet Jacques Bonhomme, so mockingly used by the aristocrats. Similar was the case of the peasants in Germany who united in secret leagues and mounted an uprising under the name Armer Konrad ('poor devil'), an epithet which the nobles habitually used to deride them. Industrialized modernity would be marked by the legendary figure of Ned Ludd, said to have destroyed a mechanical loom in order to denounce the alienation produced by the machines – thus giving the Luddite movement its name. Between myth and reality, the name became a distinctive marker, the seal of an alliance, the shield that made protest possible. There are many such examples even in the more recent past.

But even if Anonymous is, so to speak, heir to this long tradition and is pervaded by the same tensions, it also stands apart from these other examples. Its name openly lays claim to anonymity. This is a decisive difference, characteristic of today's movements, which make explicit, symbolic recourse to anonymity and invisibility. One collective of five Italian writers goes under the name Wu Ming – in Chinese meaning both 'five names' and 'anonymous'. Not only have they published a number of successful works of fiction, but they also stand for the dissolution of copyright. They have made their texts available online, meaning that they can be altered without limit, turning them into new works.[52]

Since its first appearance in 2005, in a France still shaken by the banlieue revolt, the Invisible Committee, linked to the Tarnac Commune, has emblematically identified with invisibility. It does this within its own distinctive limits: it did, after all, put its name to *The Coming Insurrection*. Published by La Fabrique in 2007, this text – rooted in a diagnosis of the present harking back to *Tiqqun* journal – soon sparked debate.[53] But it also drew the attention of the police and the judiciary, which took it for a manual for insurrection. Based on obscure hypotheses and dubious charges – including, among others, 'terrorism' and forming a 'subversive association' – twenty of the committee's participants, including Julien Coupat and Yildune Lévy, were arrested in a night-time raid on 11 November 2008. At the time, much of the French press endorsed the police account of an 'anarcho-autonomist' conspiracy. But in a few days the frame-up fell apart, and a determined protest movement culminated in the petition entitled 'No to the New Order'. Signed by intellectuals and philosophers, among them Giorgio Agamben, Jacques Rancière, Alain Badiou and Slavoj Žižek, the appeal pointed an accusing finger at the exceptional laws which – adopted on the pretext of combating terrorism – undermine democracy and criminalize dissent.[54] Only after a long and convoluted trial lasting almost ten years did the so-called Tarnac Affair reach its conclusion, with the defendants eventually absolved of having sabotaged the high-speed rail line. The Invisible Committee's texts raise the question of whether resistance is even possible within the interstices of an ever creeping state of exception, in which video surveillance, personal records and biometric identification are the norm. What can be done to achieve ungovernability? Following the path of voluntary servitude earlier delineated by Foucault, they look for points of rupture, suspensions of governance and forms of organized solitude.

What can be said of anonymity also goes for invisibility. In each case, what becomes clear is their deviation from a centuries-old tradition that had always developed in the form of clandestinity. The current mode of action, under the marker of anonymity and invisibility, is indeed unprecedented. It should not be understood in negative terms, as if merely the result of an absence, a subjection to constraint, since, here, anonymity is openly embraced – and the mask is put on display. In this lies these movements' distance from traditional clandestinity. Their affirmative or, better, performative value is to be seen precisely in this paradoxical move to appear under cover. They conceal themselves by showing themselves, and show themselves by concealing themselves.

It is, then, worth asking what it means to embrace anonymity, to organize invisibility. From this stems the difference from those, whether in the city squares or on the web, who demand greater visibility and assert their right to appearance. While they aim to change the public space, those who protest in this form also accept its conditions. They thus have to be prepared to pay the price for this, by revealing their identity, exposing their bodies, showing their faces and committing their names. What none of this does is undermine the nexus between politics and publicity.

The practices of anonymity and invisibility seek to remove pathos from the political stage. They thus bid to free this stage of the price of appearance – and separate it from this commitment. In so doing, as they expose the limits of access they also point to a new political scenario.

Is a politics outside of the regimented, surveilled public space possible? Even to pose this question may make it easier to adopt a different viewpoint from which to consider the mechanism of public space – one that seems so self-evident as to go unnoticed – and, at the same time, to re-examine Arendt's definition and its circumscription of politics to visibility in the *pólis*. But this would also mean looking further than the political architecture and its moral (should we say, moralistic?) schemas and direct our gaze towards the anarchist beyond-politics that prepares itself through the new revolts.

Masks and Zones of Irresponsibility

Asserting anonymity and invisibility in the public space, shedding light on asymmetrical relations, saying no to surveillance and exaggerated identification measures, laying claim to opacity – all this nonetheless evades an unavoidable question.

It would seem obvious that those who conceal themselves and hide their own name are seeking to avoid any responsibility. At best, they are considered cowards; at worst, they are illegals, bandits and outlaws who prefer to act by night and live in the shadows rather than answer for their actions in the light of day. Identity is a decisive criterion on the public stage; it allows for a distinction to be made between the criminal conduct of those who skirt around the law and the political engagement of those who help to reform a legal order with which they identify and of which they remain part. This criterion is also projected back on to the past, retrospectively. Thus, Eric Hobsbawm relies on the 'uncovered face' to make sense of the tangled webs of the history of Italian banditry.[55]

It could be objected that anonymity and invisibility are never truly that; not only their demands, but the repressive manoeuvres, show as much. Often, moreover, these are cases of 'social anonymity' temporarily shared by political or cultural groups or collectives. Yet masks and responsibility seem to conflict.

The debate on this point remains open. While there who are those who have no hesitation in swinging the axe of moral judgement, issuing the accusation of cowardliness, there are also those who see the problem in more complex terms – perhaps a necessity in today's landscape. The context of revolt can itself help provide some clarity. Understood in a rigid sense, civil disobedience would be legitimate only if it was conducted in the name of personal identity. It is supposed that those who disobey expose themselves to punitive interventions by the authorities, which they thereby recognize and ratify. The gesture of disobedience thus seems marked by a sense of moral superiority and permeated by an ideal of martyrdom. Yet anonymity and the mask distance themselves from this model: rather than evading responsibility, they are looking for a different escape route.

Where can any alternative models be found? It is no accident that Spinoza, the philosopher rightly recognized as a pioneer and strenuous defender of freedom of expression, was also the first to call for the right to 'secrecy' – an indispensable bulwark against the totalitarian power of publicity, which represents a hidden danger to democracy. This appeal was the conclusion to his *Theological-Political Treatise* (XX, §12), as he tacitly retreaded his own experience by retelling the history of the marranos.

Forced to convert, the marranos did what they could to avoid a martyr's fate. They chose to perjure themselves – they submitted to dissimulation and accepted an existential dualism. They moved in an extra-moral duplicity in which every face was a mask and their own mask proved to be a face. And the Jews no longer knew if they had truly become Christians just by pretending to be. Taken for traitors, the marranos evaded suspicion and kept their secret alive. They turned to escape, took refuge in non-appearance, set themselves beyond all accusation – and created an unprecedented mode of resistance.[56]

That the public stage is today studded with masks ought to be cause for reflection. There are the precarious workers who, often bereft of support from the trade unions and traditional organizations, wear white masks in a bid to draw attention to their situation without putting their jobs at risk. There are the black masks of the black bloc, an opaque mass of bodies in which rage and determination, the police bogeyman and the phantom of metropolitan chaos all seem flattened into one. But there is a surprising variety in the city squares: from gas masks to antibacterial masks often used for quite different purposes. Indeed, large numbers of gas masks appeared in the streets of Hong Kong, where a controversial 'emergency anti-masks law' was decreed and then withdrawn.

From Mexico to Bahrain, and from Bosnia to Australia, the most widespread, most popular, most frequently used one is the Anonymous, or V mask. Undeniably, there are precedents for this, even in the not so distant past. We need only recall the videos in which Zapatistas, their faces covered, read communiqués in the name of their emblematic spokesman Subcomandante Marcos – in so doing demonstrating the absence of any chief. But, with the case of the V masks, there is an obvious move out of clandestinity. This comes with the mask's arrival in the public space, where it is displayed by a symbolic 'million' – by the largest possible number of demonstrators.[57] Everyone can be V, so it makes no sense to wonder who is concealed behind the mask.

V's now unmistakeable features – a little irreverent, a little threatening – harks back to Guy Fawkes, whose name British history associates with the Gunpowder Plot. A member of a group of Catholic conspirators, Fawkes was tasked with lighting the fuse on the explosives meant to blow up the Westminster Parliament and thus strike a blow at the heart of the monarchy on 5 November 1605. The goal was to turn British politics in favour of Catholics and minorities. But the plans for the attack were exposed – and Fawkes was arrested. Face to face with the king, he showed no remorse, and he was thus subjected to torture and finally executed. Later, on the night of 5 November each year, Protestants would burn his effigy on a bonfire, amidst fireworks, to celebrate the failure of the plot. But Guy Fawkes became a symbol of the fight for freedom and rights; and even the meaning of the celebration itself has changed. Today, the reference to Fawkes is fundamentally the memory of a defeat or, better, of a vendetta yet to be fulfilled.

This shift was enshrined in the graphic novel *V for Vendetta*, published between 1982 and 1985. Child of the imagination of the cartoonist Alan Moore and the illustrator David Lloyd, the story is set in England in a dystopian future, where a fascist, totalitarian regime, similar to that portrayed by Orwell, rules by way of media propaganda. Opposed to this regime is V, an enigmatic figure whose face is always covered by the Guy Fawkes mask. Indeed, that is who he draws inspiration from. Cultured and solitary, hard-tested by the years he spent in a concentration camp – but himself also an expert in gunpowder and explosives – V combines the spirit of vendetta and the desire for freedom in a sort of neo-anarchism. Almost like a hacker, V comes to take control of the information networks, fighting against the centralized government without ever siding with a party. Pervaded by a faint 'left-wing melancholia', rather than speaking in the first person he always loves citing others – to the point of raising doubts over his physical existence and suggesting that he is rather more the embodiment of an idea. This is what is concealed behind the mask: the idea. And it's well known that the idea can withstand any bullets. But V would not have taken to the squares without the success of the 2006 film *V for Vendetta*, an adaptation from which Moore distanced himself amidst some controversy. In the final scene, the mask is worn by a gigantic crowd which overthrows the regime.

But perhaps another mask has something to say about the decisive question of responsibility. On 12 May 1797 the Great Council of the Venetian Republic declared its own inglorious extinction as it made its cowardly surrender to Napoleon Bonaparte. In those dark and tumultuous times, which seem rather similar to the present gloom, Giandomenico Tiepolo – an accomplished painter and a Venetian citizen – chose, as alter ego for his final years, Pulcinella, to whom he dedicated a 104-sketch album of drawings, almost an incunabulum comic strip. Giorgio Agamben dedicated a recent essay to this, titled *Pulcinella: Or Entertainment for Children* – though in the original title 'regazzi' should be taken to mean not children, or kids, but free spirits.

But why Pulcinella – the most popular mask in theatre *all'italiana*? A hat with a cut-off cone top, a black face with a bird's beak, an almost shape-shifting body draped in white: this is Pulcinella, the enigmatic

Neapolitan animated by irresistible energy and ready for any adventure. Dodging authority, resistant to moral duty and ever playing dumb in order to survive, Pulcinella has suffered many blows but is invincible and, deep-down, immortal.

A 'sober contemplation of the end' addressed to the 'free spirits' who choose Pulcinella as a fellow traveller, this work hardly has apocalyptic tones; it is meant as entertainment, and nothing tragic, and indeed makes sure to distance itself from the tragic. The tragic hero – trapped in pain and misfortune, victim of an error that has branded him the culprit, marking his destiny – struggles to free himself from the fetters created by his own actions, without ever finding deliverance. Conversely, the comic persona imitating his own character, moves between actions and gestures that stand beyond all remedy – as incorrigible as his continual wandering. It is not that Pulcinella does not act on the stage – just that his actions are *lazzi* (jokes, or gags). A word of uncertain etymology, a *lazzo* is an act or saying – a little playful, a little vulgar – that interrupts the monotony of the dialogue in the *commedia dell'arte*. The *lazzo* pulls open the holes in the web of destiny, loosens the knots and softens the tension. And it prompts loud laughter. Pulcinella steers well clear of playing his role in the drama. He has always already interrupted it; he has always already escaped it through some cross-street. With the back and forth of his *lazzi* he takes himself off-stage, outside the foolish sequence of events in which others would want to mix him up. How could he be ascribed any responsibility? No accusation, no responsibility.[58]

Pulcinella thus appears to take up a position in which blame and identification are suspended, in what we could call zones of irresponsibility – especially since Pulcinella is not a character but, rather, a collection of characters associated by a name and a black mask covering half the face. This mask – single and plural, solitary and crowded – is like a legion of spectres, an array of angels or, better, a gang – neither simply a multitude nor people, but the plebs. Outside of all identity, it is summoned to a higher, impersonal life.

Of course, action – which should, traditionally, be the site of politics – no longer has any place here. The *lazzi* thwart and contradict action. But it would be mistaken to think that Pulcinella is 'impolitical'. Rather, he demands another politics and points to where it might exist, in the spaces on either side of an action that has now become impossible. In this sense, it is a 'stateless hyperpolitical', which no longer has a *pólis* and no longer has the usual public space, and for that very reason is hyper- and ultra-political. Having survived the self-immolation of the Most Serene Republic of Venice, Pulcinella remains current in the time in which 'the eclipse of politics and the reign of the planetary economy' is lived.[59]

And what of 'Pulcinella's secret'? What is it, ultimately? For, in the common Italian usage, this expression means a secret which is no longer a secret, one that is already in the public domain. 'Pulcinella's secret is that, in the comedy of life, there is no secret but only an exit route within each moment.' The near messianic Pulcinella seems to be excused by Hölderlin's confident yet tragic verses: *Wo aber Gefahr ist, das Rettende wächst auch* – 'Where there is danger, the saving forces will also grow.' Translated into Pulcinella's jargon, *Ubi fracassorium, ibi fuggitorum* – where there's a catastrophe, there's an escape route.[60]

Leaks

Power hides behind the veil of the arcane, seeks shelter in the shadow of the hidden. Good reason, this, to welcome the digital wind irresistibly gusting through the immaterial caves, dissipating the smoke and blowing away the obfuscation. And, on the theme of transparency, a broad and many branched array of journalists, reporters and activists, today called whistleblowers, have in recent years exposed abuses by multinationals, drugs trafficking and money laundering, the illegal weapons trade, and all manner of humanitarian crimes. But, most importantly, it has cast political governance in a shameful light, pointing out its hypocrisy. For ample evidence of this, we need only look to the Panama Papers, which shone a light on the tax havens used by financial capital, or the circulation of the 2011 dossiers which made the monstrosity of the Guantánamo camp plain for the world to see.

The rise of these deliberate leaks, shaking the information regime and often making their mark on the global political agenda, can rightly be called a revolt. Indeed, these leaks have been punished with a ruthlessness and a bitterness tantamount to the fear that they have inspired. It would appear that such bold exposés are unpardonable. This is confirmed by the dramatic hardships suffered by three prominent figures: Edward Snowden, Julian Assange and Chelsea Manning. While each has their own distinct positions and intensions, all three have – even through their very existence – helped to raise the question of mass surveillance in the age of the internet. On these grounds, they have been accused of being spies, traitors and enemies. The fierce repression to which they have fallen victim is explained not by the gravity of the 'crimes' concerned but, rather, by the effects of their actions on the juridical-political order – effects which have prompted an ostentatious, sovereign reaction by states.

Snowden's revelations exposed how the US National Security Agency (NSA) harvests information on unsuspecting citizens through the main tech companies – Apple, Google, Facebook, Skype, YouTube, Twitter, etc. This sparked debate on the panopticon control exerted by the internet – that gigantic, disturbing web in which each individual is spied upon by the invisible eye of the screen. There is 'no place to hide':[61] this is the take-home message of Snowden's appeal to defend 'private life'. Rather different was Manning's case: she was sentenced to thirty-five years' imprisonment for leaking documents regarding illegal actions perpetrated by the US military, including a famous video showing an aerial raid on Baghdad in 2007 which killed civilians and reporters. As for Assange, his actions were of unprecedented political importance. As well as his 2006 founding of WikiLeaks, a platform that provides a space for the anonymous publication of information, he has put the very concept of 'state secrets' into question for the first time. In this lies his radicalism. Upon closer inspection, the secret is not a secret, just a piece of information which is illegitimately kept hidden in order to put up barriers around information and create a yet more lopsided relation between the governing and the governed. This imbalance itself validates the authoritarian idea that the state can operate outside of any scrutiny – a notion incompatible with the requirements of democracy itself. While it is difficult to imagine how the grey zone within the state could be eliminated and the ideal of transparency could easily turn into a dead end, Assange's action – something to which he openly lays claim, and for which he has paid a high price

– marks a watershed moment, granting the potential use of technology new meaning.

Usually those who have a positive evaluation of Snowden, Assange and Manning portray them as examples of civil disobedience. On this argument, the illegality of their actions by no means impairs their legitimacy. In publishing secret documents, they have forced the state to answer to the law and constitutional norms. In this reading, their ultimate aim is nothing other than to expose flaws in the democratic system and the threats to civil liberties. Yet such an evaluation ends up taming their revolt, downplaying its significance and reducing it to its basis in the great democratic struggles of the nineteenth and twentieth centuries.

Yet, Snowden, Assange and Manning are emblematic figures of the *twenty-first* century, and their revolt pushes far beyond civil disobedience. In order to grasp their radicalism, it is necessary partly to turn the focus away from the questions they raised and the targets of their protests and, instead, centre it on the means of action chosen, which then translated into existential and political decisions.[62] This supposes a broader outlook, one able to transcend the state borders that often also limit the faculty of thought and judgement. Snowden, Assange and Manning do not invoke the law but challenge it; they do not address the state but find a way around it. For this reason, they do not replicate conventional forms of struggle; they put into question the very architecture of politics, challenging the world's state-centric order.

It could be objected that, over both past and recent history, there has been no lack of figures who have openly challenged the law or opposed state sovereignty. Many found their place in literature or even legend and were examined by sociologists, critics and philosophers. Eric Hobsbawm's rebels, Christopher Hill's brigands, Jacques Derrida's rogues and Daniel-Heller-Roazen's pirates – 'the enemy of all' – provide ample examples of this.

But the challenge launched by Snowden, Assange and Manning is different. It does not hark back to the past, it is not pervaded by any nostalgic vein, and it is not driven by that spirit of resistance which fights to conserve its own space. Nor does it stop at challenging the schemas and assumptions behind the juridical and political system. Rather, their decisions have unveiled a space beyond the established confines, making it possible to glimpse new possibilities.

Indeed, there are reasons why the constituted powers-that-be have not only condemned these three figures to extremely heavy sentences but, above all, sought to drag them back within the confines of the system which their decisions went some way to undermining. In short: these powers sought to make them into responsible subjects, invalidating or, rather, nullifying their actions.

This is nothing short of an attempt to depoliticize these actions.

Manning acted behind closed doors and was only later identified. But Snowden and Assange did not build any walls of anonymity around themselves – rather, they became public figures. Yet, even in so doing, they introduced a practice of escape. Just as Snowden left US territory, and thus avoided extradition, Assange sought asylum, moving from one refuge to the next and repeatedly changing his residence. At first glance, this may seem like the conduct of the simple fugitive, hiding from justice in a cowardly manner, abandoning his country – and reneging on his homeland – in a shabby bid for impunity. Indeed, both men have repeatedly been accused of not being good 'patriots'. Doubtless, one can hardly exclude the possibility that they may have preferred to avoid criminal consequences. But their conduct tells us something quite different. In their departure from their homeland, in their asylum request, we should instead identify a political gesture which embodies a new revolt. For the practice of flight is a way of seceding from the state, from the nation, from citizenship.

To emigrate, to find refuge elsewhere, to seek asylum, to refuse to appear before the justice system in one's 'own country' is not to evade the Law. Rather, it is to challenge the notion that this is indeed the Law to which one has to answer – and reject the imposition of national belonging. In this lies the specific importance of their gesture, which aims to politicize questions that are taken as 'natural' and self-evident even within the most radical political debates. This is why theirs are not cases of civil obedience. The disobedient's action takes place within the community to which she belongs, and which she intends to change and improve even at the cost of self-sacrifice. But the defectors who embody the new revolt first take a stand against this 'natural' bind of belonging, rejecting the registrar's move to sign them up to a national order. Rather than settle for changing their 'own' community, they demand the right to change community. Their flight puts this demand on display. The asylum demand goes beyond asylum; it is already the transversal practice, the action of a defector, who crosses the border in order to pitch the architecture of the nation and the order of citizenship into crisis – and to do so in the most visible of ways.

Though each recognized their own responsibilities, neither Snowden nor Assange entrusted their fate to the justice system in their 'own' countries, as another defendant might have done. They did not spontaneously submit to the institutions; rather, they asserted their right to reject their laws. They invoked their pre-existing alienness from them and contradicted any claims of belonging. In so doing, they pointed to the need to unbind themselves from a forced inclusion, a compulsory allegiance. From the practice of flight rings out the implicit question: who ever asked a citizen to commit to their 'own' state? Why should anyone have to accept that they belong to the state under threat of a violence that would forcibly integrate them?

This is the violence that Snowden and Assange denounced in various more or less spectacular forms. The fact that they did this prompted brutal repression, itself making clear the importance and the impact of their actions. Emigrating, as a form of struggle, is a novel feature of a revolt that invites us to look askance at the division of the political landscape into national and state confines.

Resident Foreigners: The Anarchist Revolt

It is possible to mobilize, to take to the streets, to protest as citizens proud of their Constitution, inspired by 'civic passion' and, as they say, guided by a 'patriotic spirit'. The new forms of indignation have introduced previously almost absent protagonists onto the public stage, as in the case of women's movements, and they have opened the door to novel and innovative contents – ones which are often also global in scope, as in the case of environmentalists. Nonetheless, even the most radical expressions of opposition that invoke freedom, equality and social justice – thus helping to change and expand the public space – mostly play out according to codified patterns and take their place within institutionally established traditions.

Significant, in this regard, is their vocabulary. When this lexicon is critically analysed, it reveals many implicit assumptions and many tacit presuppositions – indeed, the same ones that define the political space as 'democratic'. Usually, the citizen shares a diffusely statist thinking, is pervaded by a national unconscious, and perceives herself as a subject of law, taking citizenship itself as self-evident. That hardly implies being extreme nationalists or sovereigntists. The appeal to state and national belonging also has its echoes elsewhere, in progressive struggles that call for reform and change by invoking constitutional values. No one can doubt that, especially in some fields, from workers' rights to the freedom of the press, the Italian Constitution is a shield which, being the result of years and decades of conquests, is proudly held up as a banner. And yet even citizens who fight against discrimination and racism, even those who call for the opening of their country's borders, do not put into question national belonging or the fact that their country is indeed their 'own'. Rather, they take this for granted. This is true both for the grander forms of collective action, from strikes to protest marches, and for individual dissent. While civil disobedience does, so to speak, push things to the limit, it goes no further than that. These citizens' commitment therefore ends up validating the nation-state, recognizing it as the legitimate space for the political 'subject'. In short, this means ratifying the logic of law, accepting the criterion of nationality, endorsing the citizenship mechanism and ordaining a state-centric global order.

The anarchist revolt does not share these presuppositions but fundamentally undermines the *arché* – the principle and order of the political architecture. The anarchist revolt violates state borders, denationalizes the supposed citizenry, unbinds and estranges them, makes them provisionally stateless, invites them to proclaim themselves resident foreigners.

This should not be misread as a claim that protests that take place on national territory cannot be anarchist, or that those that operate on an international scale and seek global objectives necessarily are. Rather, anarchist mobilizations are those which – in both their modalities and their themes – do not follow codified forms, do not remain within established frameworks, but call for and refer to a different political philosophy.

The contractual paradigm has dominated in traditional thinking for centuries, from Hobbes to Rawls. This powerful fiction is oriented towards legitimizing statist constraints and providing justifications for a closed community. It is as if each citizen had really freely stipulated an accord in order to become a citizen. And, what's more – a fiction within the fiction, this – this contract extends over time, from father to son.

To belong to the nation and make up part of the fatherland, it is enough simply to be born, almost as if birth itself provided a signature. This bizarre idea has exercised enormous influence, driving people to believe that there can and must exist some natural community, distinct from others and delimited by borders.

No less bizarre is the notion that these borders should also mark out the confines of political philosophy which, as well as not putting the contract into question, takes its cues from a community founded upon birth, ever ready to protect its own sovereign integrity. The forms of government can vary – a lot – and political theory occupies itself with this very question. But it excludes borders from its field of reflection, preferring to overlook the tangled knots of belonging in order to concentrate on the proper administration of the city. The paradigmatic case of this is Rawls's theory of justice, though one could cite many other examples in a similar vein. The important thing, on this reading, is to improve the state's internal organization, reform its laws, improve its efficiency, modernize its deliberative instruments, ensure coexistence through respect for minorities ... in short, to democratize democracy. But this political theory steers well clear of either an extension of the democratic space beyond the border or any challenge to belonging itself. The citizen here under consideration is a tacit nationalist, who judges these questions to be out of place.

Political theory cannot limit itself to the *pólis*'s forms of organization without also examining, discussing and critiquing the modes of the *pólis*'s constitution; it cannot concentrate its gaze only on the internal space and turn its back on the external. It is as if the borders had hardened, as if the notion of a community held up by genetic descent were a self-evident necessity. These questions are taken for facts of nature and thus expelled from the political field, or, rather, depoliticized. This happens systematically. But, when it does, political theory is based on a non-political foundation.

To deny that this foundation is untouchable – and instead to politicize belonging – is to scrutinize the full coercive force of the prohibition on loosening state-imposed bonds.[63] As well as excluding – or, rather, banishing – state power also includes and captures. It marks out, it discriminates, an outside and a within. The coercion is also exercised over the citizen, albeit in a different way. This is an integrating violence. Yes – as a subject of law, the citizen does enjoy protection and margins of freedom; but, already before that, she is caught within this political-juridical order, without having had any choice in the matter. The state has included her by force. The constraining character of this relationship remains in a shadow zone. Yet it is also starkly apparent in various prohibitions and in the countless ties to which the citizen is subjected. She is forced into allegiance to the place to which she is destined by the whims of birth – a place she must recognize as a property to defend and an identity to preserve. According to the logic of imputation and personal responsibility, she is summoned to respond also to questions that do not involve or implicate her, which could not be attributed to her or in which she could be said to be complicit – matters which, indeed, she feels are alien to her. Having been assigned to that place, she is called to order if she tries to unbind herself from it.

Will flight be enough? How, and where to? There can be no doubt that flight is a form of struggle, and it should be recognized as such. Within the array of forms of revolt, it stands at the opposite extreme to disobedience. Operating outside of the ethics of martyrdom, the defector – in the extra-moral sense – leaves behind the place assigned her in the state-centric order. She suspends her national inscription, dis-identifies and de-implicates herself, and puts her belonging into question. The whistleblower, who escapes together with the information she leaks, is not a traitor seeking shelter elsewhere but a seditious figure whose choice openly challenges the political architecture. For this reason, the practice which Snowden and Assange have pursued has a symbolic value, and it also lays claim to a right to flee. But it is also true that their departure from their homelands concludes in an asylum that is sometimes repeated. And, yet more importantly, both these defectors have ended up caught and recaptured within the system of states, with no exit route. The individual challenge to this sovereign power seems extraordinarily spectacular, and yet decidedly abstract.

The impression we get is that this flight also sprang from the imaginary of those who are used to inhabiting the dislocated, delocalized space of the internet. Taking an external, alternative perspective on the state-centric order, this imaginary helps to deconstruct the ties of belonging, with a disruptive effect analogous to that produced by migration. In this we see the enormous potential of technology. The boundless freedom experienced and experimented by those navigating the web may, however, lead some to believe that they can easily disregard state borders and the barriers put up around nations, whether on land or at sea. This would be to confuse the right to flee with *jus migrandi*. Yet to migrate is not a simple movement but, rather, a complex exchange of places achieved through the encounter with the foreigner. Those who emigrate do not ask to circulate freely through the planet; rather, they hope to find somewhere where they will finally be welcome. Theirs is an existential and political gesture with a subversive charge.[64]

Perhaps Pulcinella's *lazzo* cannot be imitated for long, either. It is not enough to untie oneself, to opt out, to consider oneself as having no homeland. Beyond stateless flight, one must reside as a foreigner.

Otherwise, statelessness risks being confined to the margins rather than to the edges of the city, and the migrant's bare life would fall into the apolitical abyss of the *bidonville*. Only if, rather than devoting themselves to wandering, the stateless recognize their alienness to the city – something they have in common with the foreigner – is another way of inhabiting possible.

Barricades in Time

The end of utopia, the end of grand narratives, the end of history – these are so many different ways of ensuring and endorsing the reign of the present, a time dispossessed of promises and reduced to the ordinary course of saturated immanence. Indeed, this is the time of dispossession. This absolute present, occupied by the unchallenged and iniquitous realm of consumption and communication – presentism – has been hailed as the necessary farewell to the illusory and the dazzling, to mirages and the dangerously seductive. The fiction of urgency has thus solidly established itself, while capitalism, which has no doubt as to its own eternal character, is peddled as the final destination of all possible journeys.

This dominant time, a time of domination, has perpetuated itself by muffling all conflicts and reabsorbing all dissent, instead making these into motors of its own reproduction. It has played this game with a tightrope walker's prowess, manoeuvring with transformist acrobatics. It both proceeds through a repetitive cycle and alludes to the threat of a downward spiral. Thus, even as it guaranteed official optimism, it welcomed and endorsed a catastrophism useful also for its own ends. Thus hopes of liberation have been hollowed out – now reduced to disenchanted harking back to the proper order of things, or else converted into gloomy prophecies of the final disaster.

Some have imagined that this absolute present had definitively freed itself from the expectations of redemption nurtured in the past, from the aspirations to a future justice. Some have attempted to ignore the seismic fractures, the cracks and rifts. But the subversive energy has continued to boil up in the subsoil. History is not waking up – for it never fell asleep.

In one famous text, Benjamin – again finding the symbol of time in the insurgents who opened fire on the clocks – spoke of the moments that explode the continuous, homogeneous time of the victors. Significant, in this story, even apart from the detonation of time, is the breach that opens up, from which another time seeps out. Not only does it have a different pace. It has an anarchist verticality and a poetic depth. It smashes open the unilateral axis; it breaks the chain of cause and effect. For, as philosophy explains, if history reconstructs how things went – one fact coming after another – poetry instead captures their possibilities, telling of how they might have gone. Unshackled from that chain of cause and effect, freed from that weight, each moment suddenly takes on a value which it had not previously had. Everything can resume from there, from that instant, from that single point, in unforeseen directions and through unexpected connections. This moment freely associates with others; it allies with those that had seemed lost in the past and harmonizes and coalesces with those that burst into the future. The drama staged by the dominant time breaks up, its plot falls apart, and the possibility of a different story comes into view. Pull at just one thread, and the whole fabric of inequalities that composes the profit-ruled global order unravels and comes undone.

The event of the revolt interrupts time, blows up the agenda of power, halts the routine of dispossession, and sends history off course. Unpredictable and unpredicted, the revolt explodes without whys and wherefores, without a reason. It follows its own logic – that of breaking up the constituted framework within which order's own rationales are enforced. It would be a mistake to judge it from the standpoint of History, measuring it by the yardstick of a long-term strategy of evolution, projecting it along a unilateral axis, capturing it within the pattern of the dominant time, where it ends up appearing as an ephemeral event. For such a reading would reflect the dialectical temptation to reduce the revolt to a stage, to an uncertain phase, to a precarious step towards sovereign completion. To classify it with this criterion – breaking revolt down into the immediate, the latent and the historical, as Alain Badiou does – risks introducing fictitious partitions, calling revolt into the dock and depoliticizing it. As is well known, this dialectical thinking eschews abrupt leaps and considers rupture only within a processual perspective. But discontinuous, intermittent time of revolt is also a revolt of time itself.

Why blockade a street, why stage a flash mob, why occupy a square? The line that runs from pathos to praxis, which suspends the order of places and identities, does not impact space alone. It is also a barricade erected in time itself; indeed, the multiple senses of the word 'occupation' allude to the modes of employing time. Whether erected in the nodes of circulation, in the roundabouts that regulate traffic, or in the squares filled with new, dispersed masses – it halts the time of accelerated precarity and precarious acceleration. This barricade in time may take different forms: from the explosive tumult of masks and rubbish bins to the indignant unmoveability of Standing Man (the Turkish dancer who stood still for hours in protest) and many other political-artistic performances.

This is not only a brief spatial-temporal secession. That which caused individual suffering takes on a different kind of visibility, the visibility of injustice.

The revolt estranges, putting the usual economy at a distance and casting an unprecedented light. Things are the same, yet nothing appears as it did before. In this lies the anachrony of revolt: while it is made of the same substance as the scenario in which it takes place, through its smoke bombs, its euphoria and its masks it creates an opening through which to see the gloom of the present.

The revolt crosses the boundary into partying. The carnivalesque gestures of transgression, role reversal and suspending the order of things are, indeed, rather similar. Not to mention the mask, which has since distant times linked the streets to the stage. There are many descriptions of partying as a state of exception. Power does not party: it has ceremonies, anniversaries, celebrations, commemorations, and more or less spectacular rituals through which it seeks to legitimize itself. What it cannot do is command the frenzy of rebellious emotion, the joy of the subversive explosion. Yet partying is not only excess. And where it verges on revolt, it exhibits the utopian traits of the forms of liberated life. The slave was not allowed to play the master for one day, for example upon the saturnalia of ancient Rome, only to turn back to working as a slave as usual. Partying is separation: not only does ordinary, everyday time come to a halt, but another time sets in. In this other time, the rules are not simply erased; rather, the nexus between means and ends that patterns the usual day-to-day productivity is broken, and action is unshackled from the economy of ends.

Similarly – but also with an accentuated political value – revolt does not only put habit and the habitual at a distance; it calls for a different way of inhabiting time. It summons up and refers to a shared history, so that this history does not escape, indifferent and imperturbable. A laboratory of redemption, a revolt is a time of liberation, which ties a new kind of bond even as it removes the old shackles. It brings people together even as it estranges. The revolt does not evade or take refuge from historical time, and nor is it an ephemeral means oriented towards some higher end. Rather, it is the anarchic passageway to a different space of time. Here, the future is not evoked as a prospect for the day after tomorrow; rather, it is lived already in the emancipation from place, identity and belonging, in the violation of national frontiers and state limits, and in liberation from the architecture of politics.

Notes

1 See Donatella Di Cesare, *Immunodemocracy: Capitalist Asphyxia*. Los Angeles: Semiotext(e), 2021.

2 Even Foucault tended towards such a view. See Michel Foucault, 'Omnes et singulatim: Towards a Criticism of "Political Reason" [1979]', in *Power: Essential Works of Michel Foucault 1954–1984*, Vol. 3. New York: New Press, 2000, pp. 298–325.

3 See Walter Benjamin, 'Critique of Violence', in *Selected Writings*, Vol. I: *1913–1926*. Cambridge, MA: Harvard University Press, 2004, pp. 236–52.

4 On the need to rethink the kinetics of revolution, see Eric Hazan and Kamo, *Premières mesures révolution-naires*. Paris: La Fabrique, 2013, pp. 8ff.; Eric Hazan, *La dynamique de la révolte*. Paris: La fabrique, 2015, pp. 42ff.

5 See Jacques Rancière, 'Wrong: Politics and Police', in *Disagreement: Politics and Philosophy*. Minneapolis: University of Minnesota Press, 2008.

6 It contributed to the success of the Netflix series *La casa del papel*.

7 Carl Schmitt, *Theory of the Partisan: Intermediate Commentary on the Concept of the Political*. New York: Telos Press, 2007.

8 Jacques Derrida, *Specters of Marx: The State of the Debt, the Work of Mourning and the New International*. London: Routledge, 2006.

9 Byung-Chul Han, 'Why Revolution is No Longer Possible', *Open Democracy*, 23 October 2015.

10 Enzo Traverso, *Left-Wing Melancholia: Marxism, History, and Memory*. New York: Columbia University Press, 2016.

11 Herbert Marcuse offered an analogous reflection on Proust's *À la recherche du temps perdu*: see his *Eros and Civilization*. Boston: Beacon Press, 1955, p. 19.

12 Hannah Arendt, *On Revolution*. London: Faber & Faber, 2016.

13 Mikhail Bakunin, *Statism and Anarchy*. Cambridge: Cambridge University Press, 2005, p. 28.

14 Albert Camus, *The Rebel: An Essay on Man in Revolt*. New York: Vintage Books, 1991, p. 292.

15 Pierre Victor would attack him for this: 'if a rebellious intellectual does not learn to understand worker revolt, he cannot, I think, have a revolutionary position' (in Jean-Paul Sartre, *On a raison de se révolter: discussions*. Paris: Gallimard, 1976, p. 321).

16 Jean-Paul Sartre, 'Reply to Albert Camus', in Adrian Van Den Hoven (ed.), *Sartre and Camus: A Historic Confrontation*. New York: Humanity Books, 2004.

17 Camus, *The Rebel*, p. 22.

18 See Georges Bataille, 'L'affaire de "L'Homme révolté"' (1952), in *Œuvres complètes*, Vol. XII. Paris: Gallimard, 1988, pp. 210–13.

19 Walter Benjamin, 'One Way Street', in *Selected Writings*,

Vol. 1: *1913–1926*. Cambridge, MA: Belknap Press, 1996, p. 452.

20 Walter Benjamin, 'Surrealism', in *Selected Writings*, Vol. 2: *1927–1934*. Cambridge, MA: Belknap Press, 1999, p. 216.

21 Herbert Marcuse, 'An Essay on Liberation', text from Marxists Internet Archive, www.marxists.org.

22 Ibid.

23 Furio Jesi, *Spartakus: simbologia della rivolta*, ed. Andrea Cavalletti. Turin: Bollati Boringhieri, 2000, p. 23.

24 Rosa Luxemburg, 'Order Prevails in Berlin', text from the Marxists Internet Archive.

25 Hannah Arendt, *The Human Condition*. Chicago: University of Chicago Press, 2019, p. 204.

26 Carl Schmitt, *The Concept of the Political*. Chicago: University of Chicago Press, 1996.

27 On conflictual aspects of public space, see Oskar Negt and Alexander Kluge, *Öffentlichkeit und Erfahrung: Zur Organisationsanalyse von bürgerlicher und proletarischer Öffentlichkeit*. Frankfurt am Main: Suhrkamp, 1977.

28 Slavoj Žižek, *Like a Thief in Broad Daylight: Power in the Era of Post-Human Capitalism*. London: Allen Lane, 2018. Žižek, however, has a critical conception of revolts, seeing them as lacking in strategic horizons.

29 Judith Butler, 'Bodies in Alliance and the Politics of the Street', in *Notes Toward a Performative Theory of Assembly*. Cambridge, MA: Harvard University Press, 2015.

30 On this, see Dieter Thomä, *Puer robustus: Eine Philosophie des Störenfrieds*. Frankfurt am Main: Suhrkamp, 2016, pp. 517ff.

31 See Colectivo Situaciones, *Piqueteros: la rivolta argentina contro il neoliberismo*. Rome: DeriveApprodi, 2003. Tarì has rightly indicated the Argentinian uprisings as a

'paradigmatic' case of revolt: Marcello Tarì, *Non esiste la rivoluzione infelice: il comunismo della destituzione*. Rome: DeriveApprodi, 2017, pp. 189ff.

32 See Mario Tronti, 'Potere destituente: una conversazione con Mario Tronti', in La Rose de Personne/La Rosa di Nessuno, *Pouvoir destituant: les révoltes métropolitaines/ Potere destituente: le rivolte metropolitan*. Udine: Mimesis, 2008, pp. 23–44; a theoretical point of reference is Giorgio Agamben, *The Use of Bodies* (*Homo sacer* IV, 2). Stanford, CA: Stanford University Press, 2015.

33 See, in particular, the Invisible Committee, *To Our Friends*. Los Angeles: Semiotext(e), 2015.

34 David Harvey, *Rebel Cities: From the Right to the City to the Urban Revolution*. London: Verso, 2012. Harvey also warns of the limits of these urban experiences.

35 Hakim Bey, *Temporary Autonomous Zone*. New York: Autonomedia, 2004.

36 David Graeber, *Revolutions in Reverse: Essays on Politics, Violence, Art, and Imagination*. New York: Minor Compositions, 2015.

37 For instance, the criminalization of Italy's No TAV movement, opposed to the construction of a high-speed rail line through the Val di Susa.

38 The cases of Domenico Lucano, Carola Rackete and Pia Klemp have made a particular impact on public opinion.

39 Hannah Arendt, *Eichmann in Jerusalem: A Report on the Banality of Evil*. New York: Vintage, 1963.

40 Mahatma Gandhi, *Selected Political Writings*. Indianapolis: Hackett, 1996.

41 John Rawls, *A Theory of Justice*. Cambridge, MA: Harvard University Press, 1999, p. 342.

42 Ibid., p. 321.

43 Hannah Arendt, 'Civil Disobedience', in *Crises of the Republic*. New York: Harcourt, Brace, 1972.

44 Henry David Thoreau, *Walden, or, Life in the Woods; and, On the Duty of Civil Disobedience*. New York: Penguin, 1980.

45 Étienne de la Boétie, *Discourse on Voluntary Servitude*. Indianapolis: Hackett, 2012.

46 Frédéric Gros, *Disobey: A Philosophy of Resistance*. London: Verso, 2020.

47 Arendt, 'Civil Disobedience', pp. 69–70. See also her 'On Personal Responsibility under a Dictatorship', in *Responsibility and Judgement*. New York: Schocken Books, 2005.

48 Jacques Derrida, 'Admiration of Nelson Mandela, or The Laws of Reflection', *Law & Literature*, 26/1 (2014): 9–30.

49 Thoreau, *On the Duty of Civil Disobedience*.

50 Gabriella Coleman emphasizes this in her *Hacker, Hoaxer, Whistleblower, Spy: The Many Faces of Anonymous*. London: Verso, 2015.

51 This is the problem of insiders who belong to some institution and risk being pressured into silence.

52 See the Wu Ming foundation's website, www.wuming foundation.com/giap/.

53 The Invisible Committee, *The Coming Insurrection*. Los Angeles: Semiotext(e), 2009.

54 'Non à l'ordre nouveau', *Le Monde*, 28 November 2008; www.lemonde.fr/idees/article/2008/11/27/non-a-l-ordre-nouveau_1123915_3232.html.

55 Eric Hobsbawm, *Bandits*. London: Abacus, 2007.

56 See Donatella Di Cesare, *Marranos: The Other of the Other*. Cambridge: Polity, 2020.

NOTES TO PP. 105–123

57 The Million Mask March is now an annual appointment, each 5 November.

58 Agamben, *The Use of Bodies*, pp. 247–8.

59 Giorgio Agamben, *Pulcinella: Or, Entertainment for Kids in Four Scenes*. London: Seagull Books, 2019.

60 Ibid., p. 90.

61 Such is the title of the book by the then *Guardian* journalist Glenn Greenwald, *No Place to Hide: Edward Snowden, the NSA, and the U.S. Surveillance State*. New York: Metropolitan Books, 2014.

62 This is the interpretation offered by Geoffroy de Lagasnerie, in his *The Art of Revolt: Snowden, Assange, Manning*. Stanford, CA: Stanford University Press, 2017. This work recognizes the actions of online pirates and whistleblowers as a novel development in democratic politics no less important than the one coming from the city squares.

63 Giorgio Agamben, *Homo sacer: Sovereign Power and Bare Life*. Stanford, CA: Stanford University Press, 1998.

64 See Donatella Di Cesare, *Resident Foreigners*. Cambridge: Polity, 2020.

Bibliography

Agamben, Giorgio, *Homo sacer: Sovereign Power and Bare Life*. Stanford, CA: Stanford University Press, 1998.

Agamben, Giorgio, *The Use of Bodies* (*Homo sacer* IV, 2). Stanford, CA: Stanford University Press, 2015.

Agamben, Giorgio, *Pulcinella: Or, Entertainment for Kids in Four Scenes*. London: Seagull Books, 2019.

Agamben, Giorgio, *Stasis: Civil War as a Political Paradigm*. Stanford, CA: Stanford University Press, 2020.

Amato, Pierandrea, *La Rivolta*. Naples: Cronopio, 2019.

Arendt, Hannah, *Eichmann in Jerusalem: A Report on the Banality of Evil*. New York: Vintage, 1963.

Arendt, Hannah, 'Civil Disobedience', in *Crises of the Republic*. New York: Harcourt, Brace, 1972.

Arendt, Hannah, *Responsibility and Judgment*. New York: Schocken Books, 2005.

Arendt, Hannah, *On Revolution*. London: Faber & Faber, 2016.

Arendt, Hannah, 'The Vita Activa and the Modern Age', in *The Human Condition*. Chicago: University of Chicago Press, 2019.

Badiou, Alain, *The Rebirth of History: Times of Riots and Uprisings*. London: Verso Books, 2012.

Bakunin, Mikhail, *Statism and Anarchy*. Cambridge: Cambridge University Press, 2005.

Bataille, Georges, 'L'affaire de "L'Homme révolté"', in *Œuvres complètes*, Vol. XII. Paris: Gallimard, 1988.

Benjamin, Walter, 'Critique of Violence', in *Selected Writings*, Vol. 1: *1913–1926*. Cambridge, MA: Belknap Press, 1996.

Benjamin, Walter, 'One Way Street', in *Selected Writings*, Vol. 1: *1913–1926*. Cambridge, MA: Belknap Press, 1996.

Benjamin, Walter, *The Arcades Project*. Cambridge, MA: Belknap Press, 1999.

Benjamin, Walter, 'Surrealism', in *Selected Writings*, Vol. 2: *1927–1934*. Cambridge, MA: Belknap Press, 1999.

Bey, Hakim, *Temporary Autonomous Zone*. New York: Autonomedia, 2004.

Brossat, Alain, *Tous Coupat, tous coupables: le moralisme anti-violence*. Paris: Lignes, 2009.

Butler, Judith, *Notes Toward a Performative Theory of Assembly*. Cambridge, MA: Harvard University Press, 2015.

Butler, Judith, *The Force of Nonviolence: An Ethico-Political Bind*. London: Verso, 2020.

Camus, Albert, *The Rebel: An Essay on Man in Revolt*. New York: Vintage Books, 1991.

Castelli, Federica, Federica Giardini and Francesco Raparelli, *Conflitti: filosofia e politica*. Florence: Le Monnier Università, 2020.

Caygill, Howard, *On Resistance: A Philosophy of Defiance*. London: Bloomsbury, 2015.

Colectivo Situaciones, *Piqueteros: la rivolta argentina contro il neoliberismo*. Rome: DeriveApprodi, 2003.

Coleman, Gabriella, *Hacker, Hoaxer, Whistleblower, Spy: The Many Faces of Anonymous*. London: Verso, 2015.

De la Boétie, Étienne, *Discourse on Voluntary Servitude*. Indianapolis: Hackett, 2012.

De Lagasnerie, Geoffroy, *The Art of Revolt: Snowden, Assange, Manning*. Stanford, CA: Stanford University Press, 2017.

Derrida, Jacques, *Specters of Marx: The State of the Debt, the Work of Mourning and the New International*. London: Routledge, 2006.

Derrida, Jacques, 'Admiration of Nelson Mandela, or The Laws of Reflection', *Law & Literature*, 26/1 (2014): 9–30.

Di Cesare, Donatella, *Marranos: The Other of the Other*. Cambridge: Polity, 2020.

Di Cesare, Donatella, *Resident Foreigners*. Cambridge: Polity, 2020.

Di Cesare, Donatella, *Immunodemocracy: Capitalist Asphyxia*. Los Angeles: Semiotext(e), 2021.

Didi-Huberman, Georges, *Désirer – désobéir: ce qui nous soulève*, 1. Paris: Éditions de Minuit, 2019.

Esposito, Roberto, *Immunitas: The Protection and Negation of Life*. New York: John Wiley, 2015.

Foucault, Michel, 'Of Other Spaces', *Diacritics*, 16/1 (1986): 22–7.

Foucault, Michel, *The Government of Self and Others: Lectures at the Collège de France, 1982–1983*. New York: Palgrave Macmillan, 2010.

Gandhi, Mahatma, *Selected Political Writings*. Indianapolis: Hackett, 1996.

Graeber, David, *Revolutions in Reverse: Essays on Politics, Violence, Art, and Imagination*. New York: Minor Compositions, 2015.

Greenwald, Glenn, *No Place to Hide: Edward Snowden, the NSA, and the U.S. Surveillance State*. New York: Metropolitan Books, 2014.

Gros, Frédéric, *Disobey: A Philosophy of Resistance*. London: Verso, 2020.

Han, Byung-Chul, *Kapitalismus und Todestrieb: Essays und Gespräche*. Berlin: Matthes & Seitz, 2019.

Harvey, David, *Rebel Cities: From the Right to the City to the Urban Revolution*. London: Verso, 2012.

Hazan, Eric, *La dynamique de la révolte: sur des insurrections passées et d'autres à venire*. Paris: La fabrique, 2015.

Hazan, Eric, and Kamo, *Premières mesures révolutionnaires*. Paris: La fabrique, 2013.

Heller-Roazen, Daniel, *The Enemy of All: Piracy and the Law of Nations*. New York: Zone Books, 2009.

Hobsbawm, Eric, *Bandits*. London: Abacus, 2007.

Holloway, John, *Change the World without Taking Power: The Meaning of Revolution Today*. London: Pluto Press, 2019.

The Invisible Committee, *The Coming Insurrection*. Los Angeles: Semiotext(e), 2009.

Jesi, Furio, *Spartakus: simbologia della rivolta*, ed. Andrea Cavalletti. Turin: Bollati Boringhieri, 2000.

Lefort, Claude, *Essais sur le politique: XIXe–XXe siècles*. Paris: Seuil.

Luxemburg, Rosa, 'Order Reigns in Berlin', in *The Rosa Luxemburg Reader*, ed. Peter Hudis and Kevin Anderson. New York: Monthly Review Press 2004.

Marcuse, Herbert, *Eros and Civilization*. Boston: Beacon Press, 1955.

Marcuse, Herbert, *An Essay on Liberation*. London: Allen Lane, 1969.

Marcuse, Herbert, *Counterrevolution and Revolt*. Boston: Beacon Press, 1972.

Negri, Antonio, *Insurgencies, Constituent Power and the Modern State*. Minneapolis: University of Minnesota Press, 1999.

Negri, Antonio, *Il comune in rivolta: sul potere costituente delle lotte*. Verona: ombre corte (uninomade), 2012.

Negri, Antonio, and Michael Hardt, *Empire*. Cambridge, MA: Harvard University Press, 2001.

Negt, Oskar, and Alexander Kluge, *Öffentlichkeit und Erfahrung: Zur Organisationsanalyse von bürgerlicher und proletarischer Öffentlichkeit*. Frankfurt am Main: Suhrkamp, 1977.

Rancière, Jacques, *Disagreement: Politics and Philosophy*. Minneapolis: University of Minnesota Press, 2008.

Rawls, John, *A Theory of Justice*. Cambridge, MA: Harvard University Press, 1999.

La Rose de Personne/La Rosa di Nessuno, *Pouvoir destituant: les révoltes métropolitaines/Potere destituente: le rivolte metropolitan*. Udine: Mimesis, 2008.

Sartre, Jean-Paul, *On a raison de se révolter: discussions*. Paris, Gallimard, 1976.

Sartre, Jean-Paul, *'What is Literature?' and Other Essays*. Cambridge, MA: Harvard University Press, 1988.

Schmitt, Carl, *The Concept of the Political*. Chicago: University of Chicago Press, 1996.

Schmitt, Carl, *Theory of the Partisan: Intermediate Commentary on the Concept of the Political*. New York: Telos Press, 2007.

Tarì, Marcello, *Non esiste la rivoluzione infelice: il comunismo della destituzione*. Rome: DeriveApprodi, 2017.

Thomä, Dieter, *Puer robustus: Eine Philosophie des Störenfrieds*. Frankfurt am Main, Suhrkamp, 2016.

Thoreau, Henry David, *Walden, or, Life in the Woods;*

and, On the Duty of Civil Disobedience. New York: Penguin, 1980.

Traverso, Enzo, *Left-Wing Melancholia: Marxism, History, and Memory*. New York: Columbia University Press, 2016.

Tronti, Mario, *Workers and Capital*. London: Verso, 2019.

Žižek, Slavoj, *Like a Thief in Broad Daylight: Power in the Era of Post-Human Capitalism*. London: Allen Lane, 2018.

Žižek, Slavoj, 'Some Politically Incorrect Reflections on Violence in France & Related Matters', www.lacan.com /zizfrance.htm.